PRAISE FOR

NERVES OF STEEL

"*Nerves of Steel* is truly one of the most inspiring, beautifully written, and important books of my lifetime. I am an avid reader, but Tammie Jo's story resonated with me like no other. She is a champion for not only women but for all who want to be better, stronger, and more loving human beings. Her story and life lessons should be read by everyone. She is a model of faith, ferocity, and femininity. Despite her unique and extraordinary story, *Nerves of Steel* is so relatable—I felt I was by Tammie Jo's side marveling and cheering her on through every twist and turn of her life. And what a life she has had. I will tell everyone I know about this book. *Must-read* should be shouted from the rooftops."

—Martha Raddatz, ABC News Chief Global Affairs
    Correspondent and bestselling author, *The Long Road Home*

"Tammie Jo Shults is one gutsy woman who didn't let the glass ceiling in a man's world keep her from shattering it and pursuing her own dream. As a pilot for almost fifty years, I am inspired and blessed to know her and her family. This riveting story profiles a remarkable lady with a sure destination and *nerves of steel*."

—Franklin Graham, president and CEO, Samaritan's
    Purse and Billy Graham Evangelistic Association

"Captain Tammie Jo Shults is a hometown hero to South Texans. More than that, Tammie Jo is a hero of faith. Her nerves of steel were forged in learning to trust God in all seasons—through times of turbulence and periods of testing—and to keep Him in the center of her life. In *Nerves of Steel*, she reminds us that life's challenges and the choices we make equip us to face anything with confidence and that we don't face them alone."

—Max Lucado, pastor and bestselling
    author, *How Happiness Happens*

"Most people know Tammie Jo Shults from her landing of Southwest Airlines Flight 1380. But it was quieter moments that defined her—from the work ethic she learned growing up on her family's farm to overcoming financial adversity and gender discrimination. In this deeply personal account of her life story, Tammie Jo shows us how the nerves of steel that helped her safely land the damaged aircraft had been forged from lessons learned during seasons of turbulence in her life. Tammie Jo is living proof that the real mark of heroes is not the feats they achieve but their capacity for hope, resiliency, and caring for others. Her story will certainly resonate with women who have had to swim upstream in fields traditionally dominated by men, but the lessons of perseverance she learned along the way will inspire anyone who is facing bumps on the road to achieving their own dreams."

—Penny Pennington, managing partner, Edward Jones

"Southwest Flight 1380 might have been the first time many of us heard the name Tammie Jo Shults, but it won't be the last. From a life of service to God, her family, and others—which includes navigating the rigors of the military—Tammie Jo has continually modeled how hard work and sacrifice become the building blocks of a life well-lived. Don't miss this rich, inspiring story of overcoming challenges that by their nature prepare us for what's ahead. It's proof positive that when we do what God calls us to do, He will provide the nerves of steel we need to do it."

—Dr. Robert Jeffress, senior pastor, First
Baptist Church, Dallas, Texas

"It is not often that one has the opportunity to be a hero and even more seldom does that opportunity come along twice. Tammie Jo Shults's inspirational story is one of service, grit, and humbling endurance in the face of discrimination and visceral danger. Her persistence paved the way for countless pilots to follow, and against all odds her composure saved the lives of 148 people on that Southwest flight. I feel honored to know her and to have read her story and am excited that others get the chance to see what true courage looks like."

—Peter Berg, director, producer, writer, and actor

"Tammie Jo Shults is a hero in every sense of the word, shown not only through her leadership and skill during the compound emergencies of Southwest Flight 1380 but with all she has accomplished during an incredible career. Tammie Jo is, however, more than a hero: she is a role model to young and old, in her community and across the country. She has an inspiring life story to tell, one that crosses decades of accomplishments while overcoming serious obstacles—ultimately leading to triumph in faith, family, and flight. *Nerves of Steel* gives us the real Tammie Jo and lets us understand what a truly amazing person she is in all aspects of life. It has been my distinct honor and privilege to have flown with Tammie Jo and become close personal friends. Anyone looking for inspiration, courage, and heroics will find them in this book."

—Captain Darren Ellisor, Southwest Flight 1380 First Officer

NERVES
of STEEL

NERVES
of STEEL

HOW I FOLLOWED MY DREAMS,
EARNED MY WINGS, AND
FACED MY GREATEST CHALLENGE

TAMMIE JO SHULTS

W PUBLISHING GROUP

AN IMPRINT OF THOMAS NELSON

Published in Nashville, Tennessee, by W Publishing Group, an imprint of Thomas Nelson.

Thomas Nelson titles may be purchased in bulk for educational, business, fund-raising, or sales promotional use. For information, please e-mail SpecialMarkets@ThomasNelson.com.

Unless otherwise indicated, Scripture quotations are taken from the New American Standard Bible®, © 1960, 1962, 1963, 1968, 1971, 1972, 1973, 1975, 1977, 1995 by The Lockman Foundation. Used by permission.

Scripture quotations marked NIV are taken from the Holy Bible, New International Version®, NIV®. © 1973, 1978, 1984, 2011 by Biblica, Inc.® Used by permission of Zondervan. All rights reserved worldwide.

Scripture quotation marked NLT is taken from the Holy Bible, New Living Translation. © 1996, 2004, 2007, 2013, 2015 by Tyndale House Foundation. Used by permission of Tyndale House Publishers, Inc., Carol Stream, Illinois 60188. All rights reserved.

Scripture quotation marked TLB is taken from The Living Bible. © 1971. Used by permission of Tyndale House Publishers, Inc., Carol Stream, Illinois 60188. All rights reserved.

The names and identifying characteristics of certain individuals have been changed to protect their privacy.

Any Internet addresses, phone numbers, or company or product information printed in this book are offered as a resource and are not intended in any way to be or to imply an endorsement by Thomas Nelson, nor does Thomas Nelson vouch for the existence, content, or services of these sites, phone numbers, companies, or products beyond the life of this book.

ISBN 978-0-7852-2841-7 (eBook)

Library of Congress Control Number: 2019944269

ISBN 978-0-7852-2831-8 (HC)

Printed in the United States of America

19 20 21 22 23 24 LSC 8 7 6 5 4 3 2 1

To the brave hearts aboard Flight 1380 and to the extraordinary team of professionals who supported us that day, both in the air and on the ground

CONTENTS

He who, from zone to zone,
Guides through the boundless sky thy certain
*   flight,*
In the long way that I must tread alone,
Will lead my steps aright.

—WILLIAM CULLEN BRYANT, "TO A WATERFOWL"

April 17, 2018

New York's LaGuardia Airport is a bit tricky for airline pilots. LGA, as we call it, can be like quicksand—easy to get stuck in. Fortunately, today is not one of those days, and it looks like my first officer and I are going to escape the LGA trap without any worries. We push back on time, taxi out to runway 31, and are cleared for takeoff before we even get to the end of the runway. It's First Officer Darren Ellisor's turn to fly, so I get us lined up and give him the plane. He pushes the throttles up, and we're off in a New York minute. The city quickly falls away behind us as we point our nose southwest and settle in for a four-hour flight to Dallas Love Field. What a beautiful day to fly!

About twenty minutes into the flight, as we climb through 32,500 feet over eastern Pennsylvania, this beautiful day turns ugly.

BOOM!

Something explodes like an artillery shell, and it feels like we've been T-boned by a Mack truck. A quick look at the cockpit gauges tells me our left engine is dead. This isn't good, but it's manageable. I've been practicing single-engine failures in the simulator for twenty-four years.

A fraction of a second later, "not good" becomes "not good at all." The jet, a Boeing 737-700, quickly rolls off to the left. The nose is pulled down into a dive. Darren and I both lunge for the controls and start correcting the aircraft back to "wings level." Seeing Darren has the situation in hand, I give him the plane, nodding my head and showing him my hands off the controls. Something more than an engine failure has happened, but what? A bone-jarring shudder runs through the aircraft. A second later, chaos takes over.

The air pressure plummets, and Darren and I can't breathe. The air-conditioning system fills the cockpit with gray smoke just as the air is being sucked out of the aircraft and out of our lungs. A sharp pain pierces our ears, and our heads are engulfed by a deafening roar, so loud we can't hear anything else, not even each other. The plane vibrates so hard that our instruments become unreadable, a crazy blur. We can't focus our eyes on the cockpit instruments, and an incredible invisible drag continues to pull on our 737. We have not practiced *this* in the simulator.

We need our oxygen masks first.

Amid the confusion, I have a forced moment of solitude. I cannot see, I cannot hear, and I cannot breathe. I am isolated in one of life's brief pauses, and adrenaline compresses my thoughts into an instant. This isn't the first time I've been in an out-of-control aircraft. It isn't the first time I've flown without all the information I need. It isn't the first time I've come breathtakingly close to disaster.

My thoughts are distilled to their simplest form: bad news/

good news. The bad news? With this fierce, abusive shuddering, I'm not sure everything we need to stay in flight will remain attached to the aircraft. This might be the day I meet my Maker face-to-face.

The good news? We're still flying. So it's time to get to work.

CHAPTER 1

UNDER ENDLESS BLUE SKIES

How is it possible to bring order out of memory? I should like to begin at the beginning, patiently, like a weaver at his loom. I should like to say, "This is the place to start; there can be no other."

—BERYL MARKHAM, *WEST WITH THE NIGHT*

My earliest memories are of wide-open skies. Big and blue, they sprawled over the small town of Farmington, New Mexico, where I was born. It was a land of painted mesas and arid plains boasting gorgeous sunsets and moonrises. I guess when you're little you're always looking up.

But it was my parents that I looked up to first. I remember thinking how tall my dad was and how well he could whistle. These were superhero qualities in my eyes. When I was a toddler, he managed a bowling alley and Mom stayed busy managing a house of five. Dwight was my older brother by thirteen months, and Sandra, my sister, was born a year and a half after me. From the beginning, we knew Sandra wasn't like everyone else, but it wasn't until she was nine that she was diagnosed with cerebral palsy.

As I started school, we moved to a five-acre farm near the farming and ranching community of Florida Mesa, Colorado, just outside of Durango. There Dad worked as a Caterpillar operator, grading country roads and making ski runs for Purgatory Resort. He was gone from home far too early each morning and came home far too late and seemed to always be working, but he found time to make child-size wooden guitars from strips of plywood, nails, and thin silver wire. My siblings and I took these treasures to our hideouts, where we strummed and sang like it sounded good.

Mom and Dad bought a couple of cows, a Guernsey and a Jersey that added to the cream sales. They took turns milking morning and night. Mom separated the cream from the milk and sold it, and that bought piano lessons, a true luxury, for Dwight and me. The day we got our piano was the first day we heard our mom play. It was drop-your-lunch-pail beautiful, even to a first grader. When Mom was a kid, she took lessons from Mr. McTaggart, who had been educated at Juilliard. We took lessons from the same Mr. McTaggart for three years. Each day we had to practice our piano lessons before we could go out to play.

Mom sweetened her practice-before-play rule by saying, "Piano practice will make your fingers faster. You'll be able to catch more frogs." In our home you could change instruments, but you could never quit.

Mom was always cooking or canning, milking cows or feeding chickens. She also sewed most of our clothes, and if we needed a tractor driver while we loaded hay, then she drove the tractor too. To this day, I don't know how she did it all.

Childhood was happy because my family was happy. In the 1960s we were a family ahead of its time. We lived on less, not because it was trendy but because my parents believed in living on less than they made. We ate organic, not because it was in vogue but because it was healthier and cheaper to raise and can our own food. "Farm to table" was real in our house. We were perpetually raising a runt piglet and calf. To keep questions about what happened to Pork Chop or T-Bone to a minimum, Mom and Dad made sure a new runt piglet or calf appeared as the older one got bigger.

One of the runt pigs we took under wing was cute, clever, and comedic because she loved chewing gum. When given a piece, she would pace and stomp at the screen door of our house with impatient little pig grunts, wanting to be let in. The family would gather for the show and then open the door while one of us gave a running commentary on her actions. After trotting in, she would set her haunches down in the middle of the hallway rug, put her nose straight up in the air, and smack loudly with a concentrated joy. Then, when the flavor was gone, she'd spit it out and head back outside.

When it came to chores, Dwight and I split them. We both bucked bales of hay on and off the hay trailer, mucked out stalls and spread the "organic fertilizer" in the garden, milked cows, and mended fences. When we were older, we moved sections of sprinklers across endless acres of alfalfa, swathed and baled hay, and on weekends ground our own livestock feed—wheat and milo with some alfalfa—the dustiest, loudest work on the farm. We could pick and choose some of the chores we did. Dwight leaned more toward the mechanical side of farming and ranching. I leaned more toward the animal side of it. But no matter what we chose, we had two solid hours of chores each day, year-round.

My parents gave us authority along with responsibility. I think that is why I look back at the farm and ranch work with the pride of ownership. Besides, both of my parents had a serious streak of fun in them. They knew the art of balance. There was always time made to discover, always room in our tiny house for tadpoles in a jar or an orphaned chipmunk. Mountain picnics were my family's idea of a vacation, and homemade ice cream always sealed the deal.

If we weren't at school, practicing piano, or doing chores, Dwight and I were out exploring. We dug for imaginary pirate treasure. We searched for magpie nests among the upper tree branches just to see what they had collected. We built forts between the juniper tree trunks, made mud pies, exploded dirt clods against the barn wall, and threw pitchforks into the haystack. Catching critters was our favorite pursuit.

Dwight and I played constantly . . . and we fought constantly. We had opposite personalities and wanted to approach tasks in opposite ways, whether we were talking about draining the sprinkler pipes or corralling the horses. I wanted to catch animals, and he wanted to let them go. He liked speed, and I wanted to take my time. Many times our differences of opinion turned into all-out war that involved throwing dirt clods or rocks at each other, and sometimes fists. But our arguments never kept us apart for long.

Every Thursday Mom baked eight loaves of white bread—one loaf for every day of the week and one to be eaten hot, right out of the oven, dripping with homemade honey butter. That was our favorite treat, far better than the snacks my brother and I would pilfer from the barrel full of dog food in the well house. We were never starving, of course, but we liked to pretend we were shipwrecked and needed food to survive. The nuggets gave us a sense of independence and also helped keep our German shepherd, Lady, close by on our adventures. I admit we tried a few bites as we wandered the woods of Florida Mesa. At least we knew if we were ever lost in the wilderness, we wouldn't die of hunger.

* * *

My childhood home was full of love, but as early as first grade, I started showing signs of anxiety and nervousness, especially in regard to going to school. The prospect of a spelling test could bring on such severe vertigo that I couldn't function. Throughout my life, school would prove to be a source of stress that I'd have to learn to manage. But my parents recognized I needed help even at that young age, and they took me to a doctor.

"She has a nervous disposition," the physician told them. He recommended they medicate me with a prescription tranquilizer.

Had Mom and Dad filled that prescription, I have no doubt the trajectory of my life would have taken a completely different direction. The very canvas of my life would have been replaced and a much smaller canvas with restrictions put in place. Instead, they helped me in their own straightforward way. Whenever they saw my anxiety raising its head, my parents put me to work.

"Tammie Jo," one of them would say, "I really need your help in the barn today. You can catch up with school tomorrow."

This natural reality check—how to deal with nerves and stress—started me on a lifelong emotional workout program. Putting my body in motion was what I needed to keep my perspective in check. The physical work always calmed me and had a positive effect on my mind-set. How big was that trouble after all? My mom had a mantra: "No matter what, the sun will rise and the birds will sing." Life would go on; the work would get done; the problems would pass. The following day I would go back to school and face whatever it was that had me worked up—only now I was ready to face it. And I always did.

★　★　★

When I was in fourth grade, we moved to Bayfield, a ranching town in southern Colorado. Mom and Dad had bought a sow with piglets and joined a hog cooperative, which held the promise of more cash. Though Dad still drove a grader in the Durango area, he and Mom worked from dawn to dusk around the seventeen-acre farm. For the first three months we lived in a camper while we made the old disaster of a house livable. Life in the camper thrilled me. As kids, Dwight and I ate, then scattered outside until the next meal.

The property was a treasure trove of outdoor adventure and exploration. We had a frog pond that fed into a larger pond, which had been stocked years before with brown and rainbow trout but had never been fished. Apple trees lined the west side of the fish pond, with a small dock at the south end. Dad built a raft for us out of barrels and planks. He attached it by a rope to the dock so we could fish from it or, when the weather grew warm, splash in the water around it. I couldn't believe our good fortune. This was a kid's paradise. Endless tadpoles to raise. Endless acres to roam. All the apples we could eat. The dog-food nuggets lost their luster.

As great as our new farm was, our new school was not. Everyone seemed unfriendly. The kids. The teachers. Even the fourth-grade fashion police were aggressive, appalled by my crime of wearing a skirt every other day. It was my mom's rule: "If you're a girl, you should look like one." If I wore pants one day, I had to wear a dress the next. I didn't mind. Well, I didn't mind too much. I was never a tomboy, but clothes were not going to keep me from kickball or tree climbing at recess.

Mom and Dad realized Dwight and I were struggling in school and in our friendships, so they set up their first ever "carrot." Making good grades in school had always been our responsibility, but they promised that if we made all As and Bs, we'd get our very own rifles. Dwight hit the mark, I came close, and they more than kept their promise. We each got a single-shot bolt-action .22. Dad taught us how to handle a gun safely before we earned the right to shoot it; then he taught us how to aim and hit the target. We weren't allowed to use our rifles unless Mom or Dad was with us.

The promise of a rifle to kids may draw shock among parents today, but for a farm family in 1970, it made perfect sense. For me, it underscored the fact that my parents held me to the same standard that they held my older brother, with the same reward.

We had only been in Bayfield a year when Dad received an offer to partner with a cousin on a pig farm and cattle ranch in Tularosa, just north of Alamogordo, New Mexico. It was Dad's dream to ranch full-time, so we moved again. Our new farm came with a brick house, a barn for milk cows, a hay barn, an equipment barn, a farrowing house for birthing sows, and various tie-post corrals for calves and horses. Around us the landscape was flat, with mesquite bushes and sandy soil. When the wind blew, which was often, the sand piled around the mesquite bushes, creating big mounds of sand and thorns.

We had no close neighbors, no television, and no phone. We were isolated in adobe country, but I loved this new chapter of life with Mom and Dad both working at home. To the west lay government property known as the White Sands Missile Range. Holloman Air Force Base lay to our south. Across Highway 54 and a little to the northeast lay the mountain wilderness of the Mescalero Apache Reservation. The sun rose over the Sacramento Mountains in the east, and far across the desert basin to the west, the San Andres Mountains framed our sunsets.

Pilots from the base practiced dogfighting (called air combat maneuvering) almost daily in the endless blue that was overhead. They tumbled through the sky, climbing and diving, chasing each other in simulated battles. I watched in awe, my mouth wide open. When pilots are dogfighting, they need a ground reference point, and their choice of our three-story hay barn anchored them overhead.

The noise from the jets would start as a distant rumble, then at times end with the crack of a sonic boom, which, on a few occasions, broke windows in our barn. One night we heard an extra-loud crack, and in the morning we found one of our corrals laid flat. The steers inside had been spooked and had busted out and run a mile down the road. Dad never uttered a harsh word when the noise filled our ears or caused the ground to shake. He'd smile and say, "The sound of freedom."

Slowly Dad and his partner built up the farm. In time, we had a thousand head of hogs, fifteen hundred steers, some lambs, laying hens and banty chickens, geese, and turkeys. We used our horses the way people today use their John Deere Gators or four-wheelers. Besides running errands, we rode our horses to move cattle from the feedlot to pasture or from field to field where they grazed in wintertime. We also rode the fence line to check and repair it.

I loved school in Tularosa. My fifth-grade class was a friendly group, happy to see a new face. Amazingly, we all got along. We were diverse, mostly Hispanic, but if we ever had to call each other something other than "friends," we used the labels "white," "Mexican," and "Indian." In the early 1970s in New Mexico, political correctness was still decades away, and we fifth graders didn't pay much attention to what race, color, or gender we were. All that mattered to us was whether we had enough people to form softball or kickball teams during recess. Could you hit, catch, and throw? That was all that mattered. During an inter-school track meet, different homerooms competed against each other. When it came to relay teams, I got drafted to run on the boys' team. Our team won, and we each got a blue ribbon. I don't remember it being a big deal. The boys just needed a runner and wanted to win.

While school was good, our new ranch was even better. It seemed new babies were constantly being born on the place. There were piglets, calves, and chicks everywhere. It should have dawned on us kids what was happening when Mom started looking bigger and skinnier at the same time.

Dwight, Sandra, and I drew straws to see who was going to ask Mom about her oddly increasing size. I drew the short straw. One morning before church, I made my way to her bedroom and complimented her on her hair and dress. Then I took a deep breath and mentioned that she seemed large. She just chuckled. That was in 1972, when I was eleven. A month later our little brother, D'Shane, was born.

*　*　*

In that arid land, where heat waves blurred the horizon, each kid in our family was given a pony. Sandra was first. Her pony, Brighty, was loitering in our alfalfa field when we moved in. Mine was a black-and-white Shetland mix we called Little Boy. A few years later I bought a beautiful but small sorrel gelding. I named him Peanuts, though for the life of me I cannot remember why.

Getting our own horse was like getting our first set of wheels. For fun and adventure, Dwight and I would ride in the boondocks around the ranch. Sandra was big enough to come with us, but she never liked to go far. Her pony knew the way home, so whenever she was finished exploring, she simply turned around, and Brighty would take her back.

Dwight and I would ride for miles just to see what we could see. Our goal was to someday ride all the way to the San Andres Mountains, or at least to see how far we could get before military helicopters intercepted us near the White Sands Missile Range.

It seldom rained in southern New Mexico in the summer, but when it did, it was often a torrential downpour: sheets of water, thunder, and lightning. Dwight and I would wait for the lightning to pass, then climb on our horses and go exploring. The hard-packed ground would flood, causing animals to pop out of their burrows in search of higher ground. Rabbits. Coyotes. Rattlesnakes. Tarantulas. Bobcats. Ground squirrels. It was like riding through a desert zoo. In the wintertime when it snowed, we'd follow animal tracks on horseback to discover where they lived.

As flat as our landscape was, gulches—little gorges that formed inverted mountains within the greater basin plan—lay sprinkled throughout the desert. Often a gorge would hold pools of water and salt cedars, tough grasses, and pancake cactus, a hidden oasis in the middle of the desert floor.

Rascal, another one of our German shepherds, would go into

a happy frenzy whenever I'd bridle Peanuts for a ride. They both loved a good run, and chasing rabbits was their favorite reason to take off. Normally Peanuts was a wonderful horse, high-spirited and attentive to his rider. One day, however, when I was riding alone on the mesquite-studded basin, Peanuts and Rascal spotted a jackrabbit at the same time. It was as if a starter pistol had gone off. Peanuts bolted after the rabbit, with Rascal close behind. Galloping without any fences in sight can be thrilling, so I tightened my grip on the reins, let Peanuts have his head, and enjoyed the wind tearing through my hair.

Peanuts seemed to be running at the speed of light. He wasn't out of control—at first. I think he just loved the thrill of speed and the allure of competition with Rascal. We both did. Soon the rabbit disappeared, and it became a horse-versus-dog race. I knew Peanuts could go a little crazy if I allowed him to run unchecked, so I started reining him in. I tried to slow him down, but he was having none of it.

I pulled on one rein to swing him into a tight circle. That didn't work either. He opened up even more. Directly ahead lay a twelve-foot, sand-covered mesquite bush covered in inch-long thorns. Peanuts was charting a course straight into the thorny mound, with me on his back. No matter how hard I tried to turn him, his course was set.

My heart pounded. My option to jump off had long passed. I didn't panic, but I knew this was going to hurt. I took my feet out of the stirrups and tried to maneuver myself sideways. Peanuts hit the mesquite and flipped upside down, tail over head, and I went underneath him.

When the dust cleared, I saw Peanuts far in the distance. He had somehow somersaulted, righted himself, and kept running. By the hand of Providence, I'd narrowly missed being smashed flat.

Peanuts weighed about eight hundred pounds—heavy enough to have done real damage if he had landed on me.

Though I was scratched, bloody, and bruised, no bones were broken. Home lay about a mile away. On foot now, it was futile for me to chase after Peanuts. And at that point I really didn't care if he ever came back.

Rascal was loyal enough to return and lick my cheek. We headed for home. Mom and Dad noticed my disheveled look, accented by the bloody scratches. Neither set down what they were doing, but they did inquire. Dad commented that I might be getting too big for Peanuts. The horse, it would seem, got the pity.

★　★　★

Life took a downturn when I was in junior high and my father's ranching partnership folded. Dad lost everything but one old car and ten pigs. At age fifty, with a wife, three teenagers, and a one-year-old, he would have to start again from scratch. Our family stayed in the Tularosa area but moved to a smaller farm. It would be decades before I understood the full financial weight of those years on my parents, but I knew then that times had turned tough.

During those years, my sister began to feel the strain of being an outsider at school. Sandra was not a cookie-cutter kid. As she grew up with cerebral palsy, she developed a crossed eye and walked with a limp, tilting her head up so she could see the ground ahead. Sandra had the most beautiful honey-brown hair, brown eyes, and fair skin. She was small for her age but also quick-witted, with a cute sense of humor and a ready smile.

As a toddler, Sandra understood her colors and shapes and animal names; so when the time came, Mom and Dad didn't think twice about sending her to public school with Dwight and me. But she struggled to learn how to read and write, and numbers meant nothing to her. Two plus two was a different number every day. Teachers sometimes called her slow, stupid, or defiant. Horrible names. They thought she was being ornery when she'd get up in class, walk forward, then stop and stare at the blackboard. Why didn't they see she was only trying to figure out what had been written there? Mom and Dad were swamped trying to keep the new ranch afloat, so the costs of private school were prohibitive, and as far as they knew, homeschooling did not exist. Sandra struggled on.

When I was in middle school and Sandra was in grade school, some kid made Sandra his special target. He'd wait for her where she and I caught the bus to head back home, and sometimes he got to the bus stop before I did. Walking never came easy for Sandra, and this bully thought it was funny to trip her as she climbed the bus steps. Or he'd bump her before she got on and send her sprawling on the sidewalk. Humiliated and dirty, she'd struggle to get back up. He wasn't the only bully who tormented Sandra, but he was the most predictable.

One night around the supper table, our family talked about bullying. My folks reminded us there are natural laws in life, and bullies are seldom bullies to just one person. When you stand up to a bully, you're helping not only the victim but a whole string of future victims. They also told us that silence is consent. If you see injustice but don't say something, then you're part of the problem, part of the injustice. The right not to be bullied seemed like a pretty foundational law of human dignity to them and to me.

Two days later the bully was back to his old tricks. At the end of the school day, as I approached the bus stop, I saw him shove Sandra under the parked bus, then laugh at her and call her an idiot. I ran to Sandra and helped her get up. I dusted her off, gave her a hug, and dried her tears. She cared about her clothes, and now her dress was dirty, and one of her knees had been scraped up. I knew she felt humiliated.

"Don't worry about it," I whispered to her. "Small people have small ways. And I promise you—he will *never* do this again."

Startled, Sandra looked straight into my face. She held my gaze a moment, then looked away. "Okay," she said. Her voice was small.

By now the bully was on the bus, yukking it up with his friends, sneering and bragging about his mighty deed. That day I felt none of my "nervous disposition," only total certainty about what I needed to do.

I helped Sandra climb aboard. After I had made sure she found a seat near the front, I walked straight back to the bully and clocked him upside the head with all I had. Then, making sure my instructions were as loud as his mocking had been, I said, "Never. Ever. Do that again!"

The bully and his friends were shocked into silence the entire ride home. His jig was up, and he knew it. The bus driver never said a word, but our eyes met in the big rearview mirror mounted above his head, and I saw a little grin tug at the corner of his mouth.

CHAPTER 2

GIRLS DON'T FLY FOR A LIVING

For God has not given us a spirit of timidity,
but of power and love and discipline.
—2 TIMOTHY 1:7

Late one afternoon, as heat rippled off the desert floor, I left the barn and headed over to help Mom in the garden. She devoted an entire acre to vegetables, and once the harvest began, she would be canning the rest of the summer. We pulled up beets and weeded around the green beans. She replanted radishes while I replanted carrots.

From time to time we both stole glances upward at the jets chasing each other in the sky over our big hay barn. Air Force pilots from Holloman Air Force Base were training in T-38s, those sleek, white jets with the tiny wings and pointy noses. They chased each other, racing straight up, pirouetting and hanging in space, then pointed their noses downward, accelerating toward the ground, only to loop around and soar again into the sky. They chased each other but never quite tagged each other.

"That's what I want to do," I said to my mom. I can still picture her that day, wearing walking shorts and a pressed lavender shirt. With her hazel eyes and curled dark hair, she was striking even when she was working in the garden. She wiped the sweat from her brow and shook her head. She was as practical as she was pretty.

"Tammie Jo, those people are smart." She motioned toward the sky. "Besides, you can't fly. You have cavities."

Cavities? What did teeth have to do with flying? As I pondered this unexpected objection, she returned to pulling weeds. I was a good student, so I knew Mom didn't mean I wasn't smart. She was only saying that military flight school was a challenging environment. To me that was no problem. If I wasn't as smart as the next guy, I would study until I was.

It wasn't the first time she'd been realistic with me about my future. My parents never told me, as kids are often told today, that I could do *anything* I wanted to do in life. They were too sensible to say anything that would ring so hollow. As a seventh grader I had shared with Mom my dream of becoming a racehorse jockey. Without hesitation she said, "No, Tammie Jo. You're five seven and growing. You're too tall to be a jockey. Move on to something *you* can do. Jockeying is not it." Even then I saw the wisdom in her words. Life was too short to follow the paths of greeting-card sentiments, of dreams that could never feasibly unfold.

"You can't do *everything*," she said. "Choose what you can do and do it well. There's joy in a job well done." She assured me I had lots of opportunities ahead of me. "Anything worthwhile," Mom added, "takes *work*."

A few days later, when Mom and Dad were together at the dinner table, I casually brought up the question of cavities. It came out that Mom thought they could explode at high altitudes. She gave a shrug and sent the question to Dad.

Dad set down his fork and took a long sip of his coffee, bypassing the cavity issue as if he understood my greater, unspoken question: *Can I become a pilot?*

One of the virtues I appreciate about my parents, especially after becoming a parent myself, is the balance they kept in our lives, making sure part of each day was our own. It takes time to think, even more to transform dreams into quests. I knew Mom and Dad were both rooting for me. Their opportunities in life had been fairly narrow, and I knew they were doing all they could to open up more opportunities for us kids. Reality would have its say without too much coaching on their part. Besides, I'm sure they were thinking that several years still stood between me and the start of any career. What kid doesn't change her mind a few times along the way?

That night at the table, Dad looked at me and said, "Well, find a pilot to talk to." Then he told me of his time in the Army and later the Air Force during the Korean War. He was a fan of aviation but had been medically disqualified from piloting, so he'd served as a truck mechanic.

Thanks to my parents, who neither withheld wisdom nor held me back, I could dream without fences.

I nodded and grinned inside. *Okay then*, I thought. *It's not a no.*

★   ★   ★

Flying consumed my thoughts. I couldn't shake loose from the idea of becoming a pilot. I would do this. I would fly airplanes. I just needed a chance.

With no television or telephone on the farm, I fed my hungry mind with the outdoors and with books. At first, Dwight and I were hooked on mysteries, and Edgar Rice Burroughs gave us our superhero, Tarzan. When I read *A Princess of Mars*, another Burroughs book, I found a heroine I could really cheer for.

Though I wasn't a Christian at the time, I also read the Bible because it was exciting. I read it for the heroes, the romance, and the battles. I discovered a wealth of strong and fearless leaders: Moses, Daniel, and Joseph. There were heroines as well. I read of Deborah, a prophet and judge of Israel who helped lead her people in a critical battle, and of Jael, a nomad who finished that same battle by dispatching the commander of the enemy king's army all by herself! I read and reread the story of Queen Esther, reveling in her courage and the timeliness of her place in history. I identified with the hardworking compassion of Ruth from Moab, who cared for her family when no one else would.

Books were the keyhole I could peer through into worlds other than my own. I read the classic horse books—*Black Beauty, The Black Stallion, The Horse and His Boy*. But soon I turned to aviation literature. I read about Beryl Markham, the legendary female aviator who'd been the first person to fly solo across the Atlantic east to west—that is, *into the wind*. I relished Amelia Earhart's straightforward words: "Adventure is worthwhile in itself."

Then one summer I read *Jungle Pilot*. The biography chronicles the life of Nate Saint, an innovative pilot who flew in Ecuador in the mid-1950s. A patriotic kid who longed to fly, Saint joined the US Army Air Corps during World War II and was assigned to flight school, only to be disqualified due to a medical condition. Undeterred, he eventually became an aircraft mechanic, a commercial pilot, then a missionary pilot flying food and medicine to people in remote villages. I read and reread *Jungle Pilot*, soaking up Nate Saint's life.

While such a life seemed completely out of reach to this rancher's daughter, it didn't at all seem out-of-bounds. Nate Saint had loved his country, and he'd longed to fly. In that way we were the same. By joining the military as he had, I could both serve my country and become a pilot.

Okay then, I thought. *I know exactly what I want to do.* I just needed to grow up and set my plans in motion.

★   ★   ★

I was raised by an upright, moral dad and a godly mom, who made sure we went to church as a family. My dad was pragmatic and thought the hours spent at church could have been spent more productively on the land. But Mom insisted church was important to our moral and social development, and Dad let her have that point. From our ranch in Tularosa, we drove weekly to the bigger town of Alamogordo to attend a Nazarene church.

I loved church, not for lofty reasons but because it was fun. As teenagers, Dwight and I lobbied to attend Sunday evening services as well. That was when we actually had time to socialize—during choir practice, probably too much during the service, then during youth group afterward.

Young and energetic Pastor Hayse crafted sandboards for the teenagers so we could surf the dunes at White Sands National Monument in the summer. In winter, none of us could afford to go skiing, so he took us all inner-tubing up in the mountains. Weekly, throughout the year, all the teens of the church gathered at the city park in Alamogordo for brownies and lemonade. We played flag football and Frisbee, sang songs, and listened to short devotionals we took turns writing ourselves.

Later in life I never understood complaints that the church in general treated women as second-class citizens. That wasn't the case in my church. Women served in prominent places of leadership. They were missionaries, evangelists, teachers, and Sunday school superintendents. One memorable female speaker at our church was refined and spoke eloquently about the need to live with purpose. Serving ourselves would never be fulfilling, she said. As a teen I doubted this, but with time as my tutor, I eventually learned she was right. She spoke of Jesus as I would have spoken of a dear friend. I didn't understand everything she said, but I understood her ideas were based on more than feelings. When I mentally challenged them, they stood up logically on their own, and this appealed to me.

The summer before I started high school, Dwight and I attended church camp for the first time. Mom convinced Dad to let us off work for the entire week. We left the heat of the ranch behind us and headed to the campground in the mountains.

Each morning after breakfast we went to a chapel session with skits, songs, and an interesting speaker. After lunch we played field sports and competed in everything from scavenger hunts to a teenage version of red rover, in which both teams crossed the field simultaneously, trying not to get tackled. There were always a few kids who had to go see the nurse following that game. After dinner we sat around a campfire on rock-tiered seats in a three-quarter amphitheater. We performed skits, told funny stories, and heard encouraging messages that made us realize we were all walking a similar road. Then we sang praise songs without anything but crickets and the local whip-poor-wills to accompany us. Camp was an absolute oasis.

One day we finished chapel a little early. I needed some time and space to think, so I found a path away from the main camp. I sat on the hard-planked steps of a secluded cabin and looked at the sky. A soft breeze sifted the nearby pine trees, and the sun warmed my face.

I had been observant enough through my years of playing, working, and living outside that it was easy for me to see that Someone intelligent had designed the world—the change of seasons, the migration of birds and butterflies, the miracle of life itself. Accepting God as Creator had never been a problem for me, but on this morning at camp, I came to see Him as more than that.

A Bible was open on my lap. At that time my choice in versions was essentially limited to the King James and the Living Bible, and, of course, as an adolescent, I preferred the reader-friendly one. I read in the book of James: "If you want to know what God wants you to do, ask him, and he will gladly tell you, for he is always ready to give a bountiful supply of wisdom to all who ask him; he will not resent it." (1:5 TLB)

I liked this idea of God giving wisdom generously to all, including me. I needed it! I thought I knew quite a bit about Him already, but in my young mind, God had always seemed stern. He was the Old Man in the sky, waiting for me to mess up. Surely His main concern was that I behaved. With this faulty image in mind, I was always working hard to come up to snuff, and I never seemed quite good enough. But right here in front of me, it said God wouldn't resent my asking for help. That didn't sound like a hard-to-please old man, but like someone who *loved* me.

Love changes our perspective.

Sitting on those steps, I felt like I had found a corner piece in life's puzzle. Truth, when you hear it, resonates, and this resonated. It's not about behaving. It's about believing. This was great news! At the time, behaving was not my strong suit, but I could handle believing the truth. I wanted to know more.

I felt fortunate to know what real love looked like. I experienced it every day in my family. Not all of my friends had that advantage. I knew what it felt like to be supported and cherished. My parents expected me to behave, but their expectations were for my own benefit, not a condition of their love. They loved *me*, not my behavior. Perhaps when it came to God, behaving wasn't foremost in His mind either. His one request was that I believe He loved me. This was a God I wanted to know.

That day, at age twelve, I made the most important decision of my life. I chose to love God back by following Jesus, the Man who had walked this same earth, going countercultural to prove that race, gender, and age were not factors in God's favor. He had championed those who lived in the shadows, including women. He had spoken to them and become friends with them. He had pulled them out of the shadows, highlighting their courage and hallmarking their faith. This was Someone I could trust.

Since that time I have never faced anything without a champion. What I found wasn't a religion; it was a relationship, and it was personal.

When Dwight and I came home from camp, we compared notes. He had made the same decision I had, to believe that Jesus was who He said He was. Mom and Dad noticed that we didn't argue hourly, and when we did disagree, we settled it verbally. We were kinder, more patient with each other. Decisions have consequences, and this decision brought peace to our family life as Dwight and I experienced a sibling cease-fire.

* * *

My entry into high school that fall was difficult, but I can't imagine what it would have been like without the guardrails of my new faith. Sandra's bully-on-the-bus had a big-bully-sister, a senior, who did her best to intimidate me, even threatening bodily harm. Because I stood much taller than most of my classmates, I had no hope of anonymity, a goal of most freshmen. Dances were misery put to music. Even decades removed, my freshman year is not a pleasant memory.

I avoided socializing when I could and tried to keep a low profile. Outside is where I did my best thinking. I loved the wide New Mexico countryside and the wind blowing across my face. I particularly loved the steady light of a full moon, with its bright, warm glow that cast soft shadows. Sometimes at night I would slip out of my window in my pajamas and gaze at the skies and count the falling stars. These were the same moon and stars that the pharaohs, Cleopatra, and George Washington had gazed upon. Every famous person I could recall had seen the same night sky. It gave me pause.

My days held their rhythms. School, home, chores, studies, sleep, school. But I felt anxious. I thought about the big issues of life . . . and death. My brain did not seem to have an off button.

Work became my relief valve. Again, busyness relieved some of my anxiousness. Whenever I felt frustrated or angry, I went outside and found something to do. I liked to do woodworking projects, and Dad had taken the time to show me how to use the power tools. There was always a pile of wood scraps to choose from. I would make a frame, whittle a spoon, or start a guitar for Sandra or D'Shane. Creating something has always helped to soothe me and stop my inward pacing long enough to quiet my thoughts.

By that time in my life, I was devoted to journaling. I had been helping my dad with the ranch journal and started keeping my own when I bought my first calf. The ranch journal recorded hay and grain yields and prices but also cattle and hog births and sales. *My* journal, on the other hand, was all about my Brangus steer, George. In the beginning I diligently cataloged his growth and feed costs. Within weeks, however, my journal started to wander away from farming facts. It soon included poems, prayers, ideas, memories of activities with my friends, stories of life around the farm, and thoughts about God.

I spent time every morning reading my Bible, and one morning this verse from 2 Timothy caught my eye: "For the Holy Spirit, God's gift, does not want you to be afraid of people, but to be wise and strong, and to love them and enjoy being with them" (1:7 TLB). I took these words to heart. I didn't have to be afraid of anyone. I didn't have to hide. It was in me to be wise and strong, and I would have help learning how to do it. That was the pep talk I needed.

I started coming out of my shell and leaning into life. I still didn't go to the bathroom at school, though, for fear of what the bully might do there. That was just wisdom.

The locker hallway might have been another dangerous place for me, but I was unexpectedly given a locker among the senior boys. I was embarrassed to be with them at first, but the school secretary refused to change my locker assignment. To my amazement, the guys took me in as a little sister and wound up being my protectors.

In time I threw myself into activities. We had mostly Hispanic and Apache students at the school, with a few of us who were lighter or darker than the rest of the class. Our school celebrated Mexican Day, Indian Day, and Cowboy Day. As kids, the only differences we could see in those events were the clothes we wore and the food served festively on the school lawn: tortillas, fry bread, or biscuits.

I also ran track, played flute, and became a cheerleader. I sang in plays, worked hard on my grades, passed silly notes in class, and led the student council during my senior year. I had a crush or two on boys in high school but would have burned at the stake before admitting it. My brother and his friends were always around—I liked them. Being friends with boys at that time was more interesting than dating them. I had started a mental sketch of "Mr. Wonderful" but felt no pressure to find him. I had plenty to keep me busy.

*   *   *

The first time I boarded an airplane, I was a high school junior and had signed up for a school trip to Washington, DC. It was also my first time in a big city other than El Paso and Albuquerque. I felt excited but scared. The evening before we left, I made the rounds on our farm, quietly saying goodbye to every horse, cow, hog, and dog on our property, just in case this was the last time I would ever see them. Anything could happen.

On October 31, 1977, I boarded the plane, found my seat, and buckled in. When the lovely flight attendant stood to give her safety talk, I listened hard, desperate to remember everything. Then the plane powered up and began moving. We accelerated slowly at first, then more quickly, until we were hurtling down the runway faster than anything I'd ever imagined. Then came the liftoff. The whole plane felt weightless.

I had tried to imagine what it would be like to fly, but I wasn't prepared for the sensation of motionlessness once we arrived above the clouds. It seemed we stood still as the world turned beneath us.

Later that night I wrote in my journal:

This flying business is really something else! It's as if I'm in another world, land, even existence.

On the plane, there were nine channels to listen to:

#1. Movies

#2. Symphonic Patterns . . .

I listed all nine channels.

Who knew so much entertainment could be found on one airplane? As fantastic as this repertoire was, the lineup didn't excite me as much as the view from the window, looking down on clouds with the realization that we were actually hanging there, suspended in air. Airborne.

The following year, when I was a senior, career day came around at the high school in Alamogordo. Tularosa was too small to hold its own career day, so the seniors climbed aboard a big yellow school bus and headed that way. I had signed up for an aviation class with an Air Force pilot. My heart leaped at the chance to participate.

Our bus arrived late. All my friends scattered in different directions, excited to pursue their own interests. It took me some time before I finally found the classroom where the lecture on aviation was underway. The door creaked when I opened it. The Air Force pilot, a colonel, was up front speaking. He stood tall and ramrod straight at the blackboard. The room was packed with boys. The colonel stopped talking and stared at me. Every head turned in my direction.

"Are you lost?" the colonel asked.

"Um . . . no, sir," I said. "I signed up for aviation."

His voice was flat. "Well, girls don't fly for a living, and this is career day, not hobby day. You might want to find something you can do."

I felt as if I'd been smacked.

I quickly sat down in the nearest open seat. I was too embarrassed to leave. The buses were locked. Where else could I go? Besides, I wanted to hear the lecture.

The colonel ignored me and went on. For the time being I forgot his rebuff and listened. His descriptions of aviation sounded fabulous! Flying was both mentally and physically challenging, he explained. In Air Force training, when you master flying one airplane, you move up to a faster, more complicated one. He described the different places around the world you could fly, the missions and the camaraderie. The Air Force sounded like the perfect place to serve my country and learn to be a pilot.

Today when I look back at what the colonel said to me, a host of emotions surface. His dismissal deflated me. At the time, women had been flying military aircraft for two years or so. A change of that magnitude would have sent shock waves throughout the military pilot community, and everyone would have known about it. Why he told me otherwise, I will never know.

It wasn't until much later that I realized his words were not a wall, only a speed bump. It was not my first glimpse of "no girls allowed," only the first of consequence. I had seen the sentiment posted on tree houses as a kid, laughed at the idea, and climbed the ladder anyway. I always thought the sign was a challenge: "Can you make it to the top?" Until I met the colonel, I had no idea people really meant it!

My parents, particularly my dad, had raised me blind to such nonsense. As in my church, there were no second-class citizens in my home. This equality existed out of necessity, if not fairness. Work needs a workforce.

Back at my high school in Tularosa, I stepped off the bus and headed straight for the guidance counselor's office. Unfortunately she sided with the colonel and thought it best for me to find another line of work. My aviation dreams were dashed. I couldn't afford to fly as a hobby. I needed a profession, a way to earn a living.

I suspect I am like most people. I don't like change, especially forced change. I didn't welcome this shift in my plans.

That night Rascal and I sat together on top of the haystack outside our barn, where I could see the stars. Alfalfa has a clean, rich, earthy smell that tempts you to breathe a little deeper. I told my dog the disappointing news. He was unfazed. Without ever saying a word, Rascal often helped me frame my debates, complaints, or proposals. He was an excellent listener.

When I let my dreams go in the crisp night air, it felt like a weight had been lifted off my shoulders. But it was a false comfort. What I felt that night was the temporary relief of giving up, of having to settle for second best. I needed a plan.

More than once my mother had calmed my fears about my future. When I didn't share her confidence, she would say, "God purposely created you. There's a reason you're drawn to certain things. Find what you're drawn to *and* what you're well suited for—then go do it!"

With her wisdom in mind, a new plan began to form. I wasn't as excited about this one as I had been about flying, but it seemed interesting and certainly more practical. I'd always enjoyed working with animals around our farm. For years I'd helped birth calves and pigs. I'd vaccinated, castrated, dehorned, and stitched up livestock, and I had bottle-fed and medicated just about every kind of animal on our farm. And I'd loved it.

I would still go to college, I decided, but I would major in premed and agriculture and then go to veterinarian school. How I was going to pay for all of that education was a problem I would have to solve another day.

That year in my English class, I had memorized a William Cullen Bryant stanza from "To a Waterfowl."

> He who, from zone to zone,
> Guides through the boundless sky thy certain flight,
> In the long way that I must tread alone,
> Will lead my steps aright.

Mr. Bryant had written those words during his own struggle to determine his professional direction. Like him, I not only knew the divine "He" of the poem, but "He" knew me. Maybe my first dream had been sidelined, but I wasn't going to pout my life away. There were other adventures out there to be had.

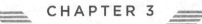

CHAPTER 3

HELP ME MOVE ON

We're an aspiring species that doesn't have
wings. What else would we dream of?
—PILOT MARK VANHOENACKER

My plan to become a veterinarian collapsed much faster than my hopes of becoming a pilot.

Cash is not the currency of a farm. Fresh eggs, homemade butter, and garden-fresh green beans could always be found aplenty. But cash, not so much. Dwight and I discussed college with our parents, understanding that everyone would have to take on extra work to make it possible for us to go. And when Dwight and I got there, we would both need to get jobs.

Dwight graduated from high school a year ahead of me but worked through my senior year so we could head to college together. We chose MidAmerica Nazarene College in Kansas, sight unseen. It had a great music program for Dwight and an excellent premed program for me.

I don't think my mom slept the summer before we started college. She did everything she usually did during the summertime; then at night she sewed clothes for me. She made most of my dresses and tops, and I bought my jeans. Mom was the master seamstress in the family and had taught me how to sew. I'd made a lot of my own clothes during high school. I thought I was being creative, but today I look back at the outfits I made for myself and just laugh. Girls at my college in those days were wearing tweeds and plaids. I showed up with cotton peasant blouses and calico prints—lots of flowers and ruffles and lace— and I loved anything with a Spanish or Indian flare to it. One of my Apache friends had made me beaded hair clips and feathered earrings out of yellow meadowlark feathers. Though my Indian jewelry and clips drew compliments, to this day my college girlfriends delight in teasing me with their descriptions of my contrived outfits.

Our family had been on only one vacation during our childhood, so the journey to take us to college was a family adventure. The change of scenery was beautiful, shifting from Southwestern deserts and mountains to rolling Midwestern fields bursting with crops. We talked about the barns most. They seemed purposefully spaced along the highway so we could appreciate them individually, each one as stunning as an Andrew Wyeth painting.

It was 1979, and at eighteen and seventeen years old, Dwight and I were fueled by optimism and hope. We were the first in our family to have the opportunity to attend college.

★   ★   ★

Those first few months at college were hard. The resident director assigned me to a quiet dorm with studious girls who kept to themselves and spent the bulk of their time studying or watching TV. Each morning I made biscuits at Hardee's. Each evening I sold roast beef sandwiches at Arby's. I told myself I didn't have time for friends, but, in truth, I was lonely. I wanted to break into the social circles of kids who had known each other for years, but I didn't know how.

I felt anxious about finding my classes, lonely for family miles away, homesick for a sprinkling of animals to add some familiarity to my day. The Midwest is known for its charm, but in spite of that I was stymied by a bit of culture shock. The idea of "going window-shopping" is still foreign to me. Why would anyone want to spend time looking at all the things they can't afford to buy? I also had impacted wisdom teeth that gave me a numbing headache anytime I laughed or chewed. Hope and optimism gave way to discouragement.

Dwight was my best friend. He and I tried to meet every day for lunch, but with different schedules and only a hallway phone in each of our dorms, even that much contact was hard to coordinate. My parents didn't have phone service on our remote farm, so when we wanted to call them, they had to be either at a pay phone in Tularosa or at my uncle's tire shop in Alamogordo.

We coordinated those calls by mail.

Mom wrote one letter each week and sent it to us to share.

When it arrived, Dwight and I would meet on the back steps of my dorm and read our letter out loud. We'd giggle at Mom's stories. Dad was bringing the barn cat in the house now for hot chocolate, and he had built the runt pig her own pen. The "farm to table" cycle was officially broken. Sandra was doing okay, and D'Shane, now in first grade, came home from school every day full of "Did you know?" questions to which only he had the correct answer.

After we finished reading, the mantle of homesickness would settle back down on our shoulders.

When Thanksgiving finally rolled around, I felt my first twinge of relief. Dwight was on a choir trip right before the break, so I packed his car for us both. He stepped off the college bus and in two steps was in the car, motor running, with me behind the wheel. We were headed home.

More than three hours down the road, we stopped at a gas station.

"Why don't you pay for this fill-up," he said. "I'll pay for the next."

My stomach sank. "I don't have any money."

We stared at each other. We both had savings accounts but no checking accounts or credit cards. We dug deep into our pockets, my purse, and under the seats. I came up with fourteen bucks. Dwight had forty. He swore the Mercury Cougar would get twelve miles per gallon with a good tailwind, but we had twenty-one hours of long, lonely highway to go, and we were going to need every penny to buy gas. That meant no food, no snacks, and no water except for sips from the gas stations' bathroom faucets. We would get as close to home as possible.

Around four in the morning, Dwight was driving on a ruler-straight highway through Kansas when the sound of a siren eclipsed the steady hum of the Cougar's engine. The darkness lit up in reds and blues behind us. I jostled myself awake. Dwight's face looked tired as he glanced in the rearview mirror, pulled to a stop, and mumbled, "Dang, I musta been doing about eighty." He rolled down his window. To economize, we hadn't been running the heater, so the autumn cold didn't surprise us.

The deputy sheriff drove a marked car but wore civilian slacks and a jacket. When his face showed in our window, he said he was off duty, but he wasn't about to let a couple of out-of-state punks speed through his county. He quoted us a figure and stuck out his hand. Dwight explained our financial predicament. The deputy's jaw twitched.

"Follow me in your car," he said in a low voice.

He led us back to the nearest town, which was small but big enough to have its own jail. I asked Dwight if he would have jurisdiction if we raced across the state line. Could we make it home?

"Nah, it'll be okay," Dwight assured me. "In the morning, call Uncle Charles. He'll wire us the money."

The off-duty deputy offered my brother the choice of spending the night in solitary or in a cell with a felon. Dwight chose solitary. He wasn't arrested, just held until the judge came in for office hours.

The parking lot was graveled and dark. I shivered in the back seat, huddled in my coat, and tried to sleep. I didn't want to waste gas by running the car for heat. Just before sunrise a young man knocked on my window. I rolled it down a crack. He was the dispatcher.

"If you promise to pay me back," he said, "I'll put up your fifty bucks, and you and your brother can head home."

I nodded but stayed in the car. The dispatcher went into the jail, and Dwight emerged a few minutes later. I gave him a hug, and he hugged me back. We didn't say much. He took the wheel again.

By the time we made it home, I didn't want to go back to college. I didn't want to drive that empty stretch of road ever again. On the farm I walked the length and breadth of our property. I fed chickens, milked the cow, and took Dad's roping horse for a ride. The whole time I was thinking and praying, trying to piece together my future. We'd already paid for the semester, and though I loved Tularosa, I knew I needed more education. When the week was up, Dwight and I drove the lonely road back to school. My parents were barely scraping by but gave us money to repay the dispatcher who had saved our Thanksgiving.

* * *

For a while things got better. One of the girls in my dorm pulled me into her scheme to go out for track. I hesitated at first, thinking I had to be invited by the athletic department. But she assured me walk-ons were welcome. We both tried out and made the team.

I signed up for the 400-meter run and field events. All those years of bucking hay bales and throwing anything from hatchets to pitchforks had built up my arm strength. That helped me earn a spot on the team for discus, shot put, and javelin. Javelin was new to me and quickly became my favorite. Track came with a small scholarship, which helped pay for my books.

Having discovered what walk-on meant and that scholarships were available to athletes, I started walking on for other sports. I made the volleyball team next and cut back my hours making biscuits and selling sandwiches. More important, I spent more time outside and around people—nice people, who quickly became my family away from home. And the physical exertion of being out on the field or in the gym eased my anxiety.

Dwight, on the other hand, decided he'd had enough. After that first year he headed home and put his mechanical mind to use. Frankly, my brother is brilliant, and I believe had he chosen to study engineering rather than music, he would have thrived in college. Today Dwight owns his own machine shop and manages another. In his spare time he teaches his grandchildren music. His mechanical ingenuity is still the envy of all who know him.

I missed Dwight terribly but decided to stay in school. My new friends helped ease the transition. I threw myself into sports and studies. I went out for cheerleader and was elected captain of the squad. I became vice president of the agriculture club and a senior homecoming princess. My senior year I earned an All-American title in javelin by placing first at a national track meet.

Things were less rosy at home, however. My parents worked every day from sunup until sundown, but they were struggling financially, and times grew increasingly hard. In the early 1980s, the prices of beef cattle and hogs were severely regulated, and it became harder to make a living as a farmer or rancher. Both of my parents took work outside the farm—Dad at a pipe supply and Mom at a local Bealls department store.

During one of my visits home in my junior year, my little brother, D'Shane, said at the dinner table, "Tammie Jo, I love it when you come home." My heart warmed. "When you're here, we eat meat," he added.

Mom and Dad exchanged glances. They hadn't wanted me to know they'd been living on baked potatoes out of their garden. They were determined to help me get an education, and I'm sure they made many more sacrifices I will never know about.

My parents are my heroes and always will be. As I approached graduation, however, it became clear that, in spite of all their efforts, affording vet school was out of the question. With my sports scholarships ending and student loans mounting, I needed to be honest with myself. It was time to get serious about life after college.

★   ★   ★

Janice Blakeman was one of my college friends. We bonded over our shared sense of humor. We could laugh at everything, and we could laugh at nothing. In the fall of our senior year, Janice announced her plans to go into the Air Force as a nurse. All three of her brothers were Air Force pilots. She mentioned that her older brother was getting his wings and invited me to join her for the ceremony. I was happy to go, to see all of the military pomp and circumstance at Vance Air Force Base in Enid, Oklahoma, and I applauded with everybody else when Janice's brother received his wings. But my mind was in another world.

There, right in front of me, sitting in the graduating class was . . . a girl.

One newly minted female pilot.

My mind buzzed with excitement. This woman had made it! But how? She must be some brilliant rocket scientist destined to become an astronaut, I thought. Or maybe—just maybe—the military door wasn't as firmly shut to women as I had been told.

After the ceremony I made my way through the crowd to her, introduced myself, and asked how she'd gotten into pilot training. She explained she'd gone through her college's Reserve Officer Training Corps (ROTC) program. Because I was about to graduate, ROTC wasn't an option for me. Once again, my heart sank.

On the trip back to Kansas, Janice suggested that I get a commission as an officer and then apply to flight school. That night I could barely sleep. The idea of becoming a pilot seemed attainable. I rolled the possibility around and around inside my head, and it seemed solid. Another woman had become an Air Force pilot. If she could do it, then maybe I could too.

Before I graduated, I spoke with an Air Force recruiter. His answer was polite but firm. He said the Air Force wasn't interested in me. End of story.

I waited awhile and spoke with a different Air Force recruiter. He was also polite and also just as firm. No way, no how. Wasn't ever going to happen.

The Air Force was actively recruiting pilots. I saw an ad in the newspaper, clipped it out, and took it with me when I made my third visit to the Air Force recruiter's office.

He shook his head at me and said, "If you have a brother with a degree who wants to be a pilot, bring him in. We aren't accepting applications from girls."

I heard the Army had pilots, so I spoke with them. They politely said I was not a fit and closed the door.

Then Janice pointed me toward the Navy. I didn't know much about the Navy. In my mind the Navy meant oceans, and I'd only lived in landlocked states. I don't remember if I'd ever seen a real ship, but I figured I didn't have anything to lose.

The naval recruiter was more amiable than any recruiter I'd met. He invited me to take the Armed Services Vocational Aptitude Battery (ASVAB), the standardized military entrance exam. The test is lengthy, comprising roughly eight hundred questions about math, auto and shop information, electronics, general science, mechanical comprehension, and aviation aptitude. I took the test and missed passing by six questions. The recruiter informed me that I could study and take the test again in six months, so I bought a book to learn how to prepare for the ASVAB.

After graduating from college, I took the test again in El Paso and passed. The enlisted recruiter said, "Great job! You'll just need to come back when the officer recruiter can process your paperwork." He was all smiles.

Wow! I was so happy. I told my friends, "I'm in!"

I returned to have my paperwork processed by the appropriate naval recruiter. "We don't need girls," he told me. "I'm not processing your paperwork."

My brow furrowed. "But the other recruiter said I scored high enough," I said.

"You scored high enough for a guy," the man said, "but not for a girl."

I was crestfallen. How would I ever get past this guy/girl stuff? What did a girl have to do to serve her country as a pilot?

I didn't know what else to try. Once again I cut the military out of my plans for the future.

* * *

My parents had moved temporarily to Roswell, New Mexico—a town carved out of dirt by wind—because Sandra needed a school that was there. I didn't know what else to do with my life, so I packed up and went with them.

One solid job lead emerged with a large agricultural company in Iowa. They offered to pay for a plane ticket so I could come up for the interview. I mentioned I was interested in learning to fly someday and asked the hiring manager if I could have the money for an airplane rental and an instructor instead. To my surprise he said yes, so I located an instructor near Roswell and rented a single-engine Cessna to take me to my interview.

While en route the instructor talked to me about flying. My view from above the clouds was a little slower and a little lower this time. It took quite a while to reach our destination in that small plane, and it turned out the job offer was to feed pigs. Pig farming is honest work. My dad had been a pig farmer on and off for much of his life, and I'd done that enough myself to be qualified. I said I'd consider it.

On the way home the instructor stopped talking for a while. As we flew back over the great plains of Kansas, I felt the steadiness of the engine and my breathing deep within me. By the time we glimpsed the majestic mountains outside Santa Fe, I knew I couldn't go back to feeding pigs. I would keep looking.

In Roswell I substitute taught while I looked for a full-time job. Days of job searching turned into weeks. Then months. Then a year. I invested in flute lessons so I could keep up my music and my sanity. I felt aimless and uncertain but not depressed. I was confident that God would eventually show me what I needed to discover.

Eventually I got plugged into a church and became the children's church leader. I had forgotten how good it felt to invest time and energy in other people, especially children. This group of pre-K through third graders returned my heart to a happy place. Among other things, we put on a musical that was picked up by the local television station.

About this time the matchmakers in my life stepped in to "help."

When I was little, I'd thought I would marry my dad, then

Tarzan, then Zorro. By college the mask had come off of my idea of Mr. Wonderful. Though he remained faceless, the framework of a man who was more modern but had the same good character began to take shape in my mind. Like my career, he seemed to be taking his time presenting himself to me. At work and at church, I met some wonderful men, but they weren't "him."

During this time, I was briefly engaged—until my fiancé and I realized we were headed toward marriage for all the wrong reasons. Rather than acknowledging the truth about who we were and what our hearts were telling us, we were trying to make the people around us happy. After all, marriage was what people in their twenties were supposed to do, right?

Early one morning my dad was out on the tractor in a field he had leased. I shuffled across the furrows to where he worked. He nodded, and I climbed aboard and sat on the fender.

"Dad!" I hollered over the *chug, chug, chug.* "I don't want to do this."

He understood I was talking about getting married. He didn't stop the tractor, and he didn't have a long conversation with me. He just shot me a knowing look and hollered back, "Well, don't."

Dad always knew how to cut through the dust clouds. My fiancé and I broke our engagement.

Time continued to pass. I kept working as a substitute teacher, even teaching my little brother's fifth-grade class on and off. During that long season, D'Shane became a bright spot in my life. He'd grown up a lot in those years I'd been away at college, and I completely enjoyed getting to know him again. This time with my family was not what I had planned, but it was wonderful.

I signed up for flight lessons. Perhaps I was romanticizing flying. I thought that putting in the hard work of actually doing it would help me let go.

On April 7, 1984, I drove out to Great Southwestern Aviation, where Mr. Russ Reece gave me my first lesson. I loved it! Over the course of the next few weeks, I took a few more lessons, but one day as I drove home, I let some common sense settle in. I was the only person in my family with a college education and the only one without a real job. An expensive hobby was the last thing on my list of "to dos" in life. It was time to get real.

For a while I worked as a receptionist for McClellan Oil Corporation. I think I got the job because one of the engineers was a track-and-field fan and noticed I was a javelin thrower. There was no future for me in this job, but it gave me an income and an example of how a good company is run.

I also kept working with the kids at church. Mom saw how I enjoyed children and suggested I get my teaching credentials. The plan made sense. The oil company gave me a sweet farewell party, I took out more loans, and I packed everything I owned into my old Pinto. Then I drove to Silver City to begin graduate studies at Western New Mexico University.

My studies there progressed well, but I still had a yearning deep in my heart. The desire to fly nagged me and wouldn't let go. I wasn't about to trouble God again by asking Him to help me fly. I'd already asked Him, already banged on as many doors as I could, but the answer always seemed to be no. Besides, I had nothing to complain about. My life was going better than ever. In addition to my graduate studies, I was busy with a job as a photographer for the alumni paper. So I changed my prayers. Now, instead of praying, "Help me fly," I prayed, "Help me move on." Throughout that first semester of graduate school, I prayed that prayer.

One day toward the end of the semester, it dawned on me

that God was not saying yes to this prayer either. I had spent a minimal amount of time pouting during the past two years. I hadn't wallowed in disappointment or refused to stay active doing what I could. Even so, the lure of flying wasn't going away. It was still strong, and in unguarded moments I realized that it was even growing. Why could I not get past it?

Often in those months my mom's wisdom came back to me: *God purposely created you. There's a reason you're drawn to certain things. Find what you're drawn to and what you're well suited for—then go do it!* My responsibility wasn't to worry about my future. It was to trust in God and work hard to be ready when He sent opportunities my way. I had never believed it would do me any good to sulk in an office or a classroom because I couldn't sit in a cockpit, and I wasn't about to start now.

After nearly two years without a clear direction, I tried one last time.

I called the Navy recruiter in Albuquerque because I'd be passing through that city on my way home for break. He was new, and I'd never spoken with him before. I explained how I'd wanted to become a pilot through the military, how I'd taken and passed the ASVAB but was told I'd scored high enough for a guy, but not for a girl.

"Wait a minute," he said. "The Navy doesn't have different ASVAB requirements for men and women. Give me your Social Security number and we'll get to the bottom of this."

I gave him my number, and he looked up my scores.

"Your scores are terrific," he said. "Come by here before you head back to school in January. We'll get all your paperwork and application completed and turned in."

This recruiter made good on his promises. In early January

1985, my application packet for the Navy was at last completed, submitted, and approved. Just two months later I found myself in Pensacola, Florida, ready for my first step on a long road: Aviation Officer Candidate School.

CHAPTER 4

YOU'RE IN THE NAVY NOW

On your face, maggots!

—AOCS DRILL INSTRUCTOR

In the 1982 movie *An Officer and a Gentleman*, Richard Gere's character, Zack Mayo, goes through Aviation Officer Candidate School (AOCS), which is why my friends at Western New Mexico University rented the video for us to watch the night before I left grad school. As it turned out, that movie got a lot right. AOCS is a fourteen-week program in which college graduates can earn a naval commission without passing through the

United States Naval Academy or ROTC. Every branch of the military has its own officer candidate school (OCS), but AOCS is the Navy's boot camp for those who want to fly.

I had orders to report to Naval Air Station (NAS) Pensacola on a Sunday, so I left early enough to drive from New Mexico to Florida and arrive on the Friday before. Dwight had bought four new tires for my car because he wanted to make sure I got there safely. Mom made the road trip with me to keep me company and, I found out later, to soothe her nerves. She was anxious to the point of tears about me joining the military, but she hid it well. On Saturday we enjoyed going through the naval aviation museum on base; then I took Mom to the airport to catch a plane home.

Before checking in to AOCS on Sunday morning, I attended a church on base. Church continued to be a constant that kept me centered and grounded, and if there ever was a day that I needed centering and grounding, it was that day in March 1985. Though I was finally on the path to becoming a pilot, I faced it with some trepidation. I was standing on the brink of the unknown.

At the church service a young man sat beside me. He struck up a conversation, remarking that he hadn't seen me there before. I explained I'd come to Pensacola for AOCS, which surprised and, I think, amused him. He told me he'd just finished the program himself, then offered helpful advice about where to park when I checked in. His kindness eased my nerves a bit.

After church I drove across to the AOCS check-in building and parked my 1970 Mustang right beside it, where the gentleman at church had recommended. I shut the car door behind me and paused for a moment, gazing at the beautiful, old redbrick buildings. The grounds of NAS Pensacola felt like an elite college campus, with lawns manicured like putting greens and buildings smartly trimmed in white. Catty-corner across the street was a polished F-4 Phantom. Its nose was pointing right at the check-in building, as if to say, "If you want to fly Navy, enter here." My pulse kicked up a notch as I hauled my luggage from the car and gathered my papers.

The building, I would soon learn, was referred to as a battalion and was much like a dormitory. I walked up the steps and into the lobby, where a group of men in khaki uniforms, engaged in various tasks, were chatting with one another as they worked. One of them greeted me politely.

"Afternoon, ma'am. Help you find someone?" he asked, glancing around the busy room.

"No, actually"—I held out my paperwork—"I'm here to check in."

My announcement caught the ears of the other men, and the casual atmosphere shifted. One of them shouted, "Secure your luggage to the—!" while another simultaneously barked, "—bulkhead!" Soon all the men had dropped whatever they were doing and joined in, all shouting in unison, and all shouting the same jumbled words: "secure!" "bulkhead!" "luggage!" "your!" I had no idea what it meant to secure something, and I was equally at a loss over the definition or whereabouts of a bulkhead.

When there was a lull in the shouting, I made the mistake of saying calmly, "If you would quit yelling, I could understand you." That only poured gasoline on the fire, and the shouting doubled in volume and confusion. "yourluggagetobulkhead-secure!" Somehow, I determined that a bulkhead must be a wall. Setting my luggage against the wall was my first order.

When my luggage was in its proper place, the shouting paused, so I pointed outside and asked if I should move my car to a parking lot now that I'd dropped off my suitcase. The group looked out the window in disbelief, and a fresh barrage of screaming ensued. It quickly became clear I'd parked on a road used only for marching, and my parking there was tantamount to high treason. Apparently not even admirals parked next to the battalion. I'm sure the guy I had met at church was somewhere laughing uncontrollably. After all the pranks I've been subjected to over the years, that one still cracks me up.

I shook off the group, went and parked my car some distance away in the seawall parking lot, and ran in my high heels back to the battalion.

One of the khaki-clad men directed me by shouts to my room. I started walking in that direction when someone else yelled, "Stupid! Stop! Stoo-pid!" *How rude to call someone stupid*, I thought, particularly when the yelling continued: "Halt! Stoo-pid! Quit walking! Stop! Idiot!" Later I was told they were yelling at me. I didn't ask why.

My room looked prisonlike with its battleship-gray furniture, oversize metal lockers, and naked twin beds set up for four candidates. Our class was composed of about seventy-five candidates, but only three of us were women—Blewey, McCopin, and me—the highest number of women in an AOCS class to date. To commemorate the occasion, Class 1-6-8-5 became known as the Class of Girls. When the three of us learned this, we were pretty sure our seventy-two male classmates would not be pleased.

★ ★ ★

The next morning at 5:00 a.m., we awoke to the earsplitting ruckus of metal trash cans careening down the hallway. "Get up, you filthy maggots!" bellowed our drill instructor. This was followed by a string of the most creative name-calling I'd ever heard. We were pigs, knuckleheads, worms, and worse. The candidate officers, seniors in the program, had forewarned us of this moment. When the drill instructor announced his arrival, we were to "fall out" into the hallway and stand at attention against the bulkhead, and we had better do it quickly.

I guess we weren't quick enough.

The drill instructor, Staff Sergeant Carney, informed us that we were the worst excuses for candidates he had ever seen. In his life. In the history of officer candidate school. Not only that, the way we were standing at attention was a disgrace to the United States Navy.

"On your face, maggots!" he ordered, and we dropped to a push-up position. We didn't do that quickly enough either, so we practiced a few dozen more times. He instructed us in the finer points of every exercise you can imagine: push-ups, leg lifts, jumping jacks, squat thrusts, lunges, and high stepping. You name it, we did it. "Get 'em!" was an order to begin the assigned exercise *right now*. For example, "Leg lifts, get 'em!" And we did leg lifts to the point of exhaustion. The whole routine was called PT, for *physical training*, and he used it as a verb.

Staff Sergeant Carney, United States Marine Corps, was fit, his uniform was crisp and spotless, and his countenance was grim. He spoke perfectly clear English at the rate of a speeding freight train, insulting and demeaning us mercilessly and with a sharp wit. Occasionally a candidate would lose his military bearing and laugh, which I expect was our drill instructor's secret goal. Any excuse to PT us was a good excuse for him to scream, "On your face, maggots!"

He wanted us to do everything in a specific way. *His* way. That morning he explained his definition of "attention to detail."

If there was an overarching theme to AOCS, that was it. Every day for the next fourteen weeks, we were trained to pay attention to every single detail of every single thing we did. There was a proper way to stand at attention, to salute, to hold a fork, to do a push-up, to make a bed, to wear a uniform, and even to lace up shoes—outboard over inboard. Every detail mattered.

At the time, I saw these demands as just another hurdle I had to clear to *become* a Navy pilot. I would later appreciate that attention to detail was an integral part of *being* a Navy pilot and that paying attention to the details can save lives.

Our drill instructor never outright swore at us and never used any vulgarisms for female body parts, at least not around our class. He must have been prepped for the Class of Girls because I heard that this was not the case for other classes. Every other derogatory word or concept, however, was fair game, and we soon found out that "girls!" and "ladies!" were also derogatory terms. The drill instructor leaned heavily on these and directed them most often at the guys in our class.

Within the first day or two, we were issued uniforms called "poopy suits," which consisted of heavy, green, long-sleeved shirts and pants and metal helmets that I'm pretty sure had seen service in World War II. They were dirty, dented, and stank to high heaven, but that was the least of my concerns. As much as we were sweating, no one could tell whether the stink came from the helmets or our bodies.

One of the battalions had a trampled-down courtyard with one solitary, feeble rosebush in the middle that reminded me of Charlie Brown's Christmas tree. Our first invitation to this oasis came from our drill instructor over the battalion PA.

"Class 1-6-8-5, meet me in the Rose Garden. And don't make me wait on you, ladies!"

We all bolted out of our rooms and beat feet to the Rose Garden. As I ran at full speed to get into formation, I passed behind the staff sergeant. He shouted, "Well, excuse me!"

Thinking he was being polite, I respectfully answered, "No, you're fine," then found my place in line and stood at attention.

Staff Sergeant Carney met me face-to-face and planted the brim of his campaign hat (which always made me think of Smokey the Bear) in the middle of my forehead. Scowling, he proceeded to explain, at the top of his lungs, that proper military bearing dictated I should have said, "By your leave, sir," as I passed behind him. He used my "egregious display of disrespect" as an excuse to PT the whole class until the cows came home. They didn't come home for a while that day.

When it was time for our military haircuts, we double-timed it over to a nearby building, where the staff sergeant shouted at us to line up. The men were placed first in line, arranged from tallest to shortest. The women were at the back, again tallest to shortest. My tall frame stood out at the short end of the lineup of men.

"You wreck the formation, Everest!" the drill instructor shouted at me.

Of course I did.

Inside the building we fanned out into six lines facing six grinning barbers, each buzzing away happily on the head of a new candidate. Three of the men in my battalion quit right there, taking the drop-on-request (DOR) option. After they were gone, man after man was shaved bald. The barbers were quick; before I knew it, I had been sheared like a sheep. When I saw my shoulder-length hair on the floor, I simply thought, *Whatever.* It would grow back, and no way was I going to cry over lost hair, even if I did look like an alien.

We went straight from the barber to have our ID tags made. I mailed an extra picture home to my parents. Weeks later, when I was able to call home for the first time, Mom said to me, "Honey, you look like a POW. Please don't send any more pictures until your hair grows out. It's scaring your younger brother."

★ ★ ★

Each day a different person served as our class's section leader. The task was doled out alphabetically, and since my maiden name is Bonnell, I was up first. The section leader's job was to march the class in an orderly fashion between the events of the day. I'd been in the marching band for several years in high school, so marching wasn't a problem for me, but the military used traditional call-and-response cadences called jodies to keep a group marching in step. I didn't know even one jody, not even the classic that begins, "I don't know, but I've been told . . ." I did, however, remember lots of cheers from my days as a college cheerleader.

The drill instructor left me in charge. I knew where we needed to be and when we had to be there, so I marched to the front of the formation, moved to the side, and called out, "Forward, march." Once we were moving, I called out: "All right! All right! All right!"

The class yelled, "All right!"

"Okay! Okay! Okay!"

"Okay!"

"All right!"

"All right!"

"Okay!"

"Okay!"

And together we all shouted, "Navy all the way!"

When the drill instructors heard our cheer, they started flooding out of the battalion. I got through the routine a couple of times before they surrounded me, drowning out my voice with their own shouts. Staff Sergeant Carney fired me on the spot.

I was never allowed to serve as section leader again, and from that moment on, I was a target. For the rest of my time in AOCS, not one drill instructor had a problem pulling me out of ranks and ordering me to do additional PT while recounting my unforgivable sin of marching a class of warriors with a college cheer.

I tried to take it all in stride. In a strange way the punishment was comforting. I felt like part of the gang anytime I was being screamed at. Soon enough the drill instructors would be screaming at someone else. The whole point of military boot camp is to break down individuals and build them back up as part of a team. It was all part of the game, and I was happy to be in it.

A few weeks into AOCS, when Easter morning dawned bright, the other female candidates and I slid "Happy Easter" cards under everybody's door. Our classmates seemed to like them. I think we were all craving a little taste of the outside world. Our drill instructor, on the other hand, blew a gasket. He ordered all three of us into his office, where he PTed us for the next hour. After we were completely wrung out, he shouted: "There will be no more sweet little cards passed around. We are training naval aviators!"

But later in the program, on a visit to his office, I noticed his Easter card under the plexiglass cover on his desk.

★ ★ ★

"Mom, please stop sending cookies."

I made my plea during a call home one day. Mom's homemade cookies, sent weekly with the best of intentions, were getting me in trouble with my classmates.

Every day after completing either the obstacle course or the cross-country course or whatever PT they had planned, we'd go straight to the battalion hallway for mail call, exhausted and sweaty. Anyone who received a package had to open it on the spot for examination, and anyone who received food had to *eat* it on the spot, though eating sweets was the last thing any of us wanted to do after PTing all afternoon in the Florida heat. My generous mom would send a huge box of cookies with enough for the whole class, and the drill instructor made everyone eat his share.

After I explained, Mom just said, "Okay," and that was that.

When the next week rolled around and I received another box from home, everyone groaned. It was heavy, and I was worried. But it contained only a letter, some magazines Mom thought I'd like to look at, and a few other inedible items. Sending Mom a silent thank-you, I tossed the box into my room. It landed on the ground with a strangely loud thump.

What on earth? I thought, but I would have to investigate that later. We were headed to chow.

"That box felt heavy," I said to one of my roommates. She looked at me like I was imagining things.

I couldn't make sense of it until I got back from supper and had a closer look. As I ran my fingers around the inside of the box, I found an odd seam in the cardboard. I tugged at it, peeling it away to reveal a stash of dozens of cookies. Mom had built a false bottom into the box to hide them!

Her creativity made us all laugh. From then on my classmates and I ate the cookies when we could actually enjoy them.

When we weren't eating cookies, we were just trying to survive the PT sessions, academics, military drills, and learning how to march with a rifle. The drill instructor thrashed us all alike, though sometimes the girls got special attention because we "ruined" his formation. Overall, when it came to us women, no one was particularly welcoming or hostile, kind or hateful. For the most part, we were simply part of the gang.

The only real shadow that fell over that time came during my physical. The exam was given by a team of doctors from the Naval Aviation Medical Institute (NAMI). NAMI's primary purpose, or so it seemed, was to find a medical reason to disqualify officer candidates. This disqualification was called a "NAMI Whammy," and I appreciated the reason for it, but that didn't make the exam any less stressful. The physical was thorough and covered every portion of the body. Women got the same treatment as the guys, with the addition of a gynecological exam.

The doctor who did our exams was disgruntled at having to do the women's physicals. When I met him, he announced to me, "This is beyond the scope of my duty." Things went downhill from there. The exam took place behind closed doors, but when he finished the gynecological portion, he threw open the door and walked out while I was still lying exposed on the table. Right outside that door was the waiting room and the rest of my class. Thanks to the annoyed physician, I had just flashed them all.

The nurse who was with me apologized profusely as she scrambled around the table to shut the door. I murmured my thanks, quickly finished dressing, and waded out into a sea of men. To their credit, my classmates avoided my eyes and didn't say a thing. Whether this was out of respect or embarrassment,

I don't know, but I was glad they allowed me to put it behind us and move on.

It's much more likely that such an incident today would be handled with the outrage it deserves. But back then I had no delusion that sending a complaint up the chain of command would call that doctor to account. It would have only jeopardized my chance to stay in the program, and I wasn't willing to risk that.

Physically, I kept up with my classmates. College athletics had me in good shape entering the program, so I could hold my own when it came to knocking out push-ups and leg lifts. When we ran as a group, I was in the pack. I never finished in first place, but I never finished last either. With each new day came more PT sessions, classes, and military drills, as well as constant reminders that our "attention to detail" was unsatisfactory. This led, of course, to more PT sessions. It was a bit like a merry-go-round that seemed to start and end and start again with "On your face, maggots!" This was all just part of the program, and I found that intentionally putting my mind on something else helped me (and my aching muscles) get through it.

My survival motto came from a verse in the Bible, Isaiah 50:7. I would repeat it over and over to myself.

> For the Lord GOD helps Me,
> Therefore, I am not disgraced;
> Therefore, I have set My face like flint,
> And I know that I will not be ashamed.

Even with all the demands of AOCS, I continued to keep my journals. They were a slice of normal in my life. I often headed my entries with the date, the words *year of my Lord*, and began with "Heavenly Father . . ." In those pages I told God about the high points of the day, no matter how small. I told Him about a time I was able to bring a smile to my drill instructor's face and a time when I aced a test. I also told Him about the lows, like the incident with the NAMI doctor. Then I left them in His hands. I found that was the best way to keep them from rolling around and festering in my mind. The practice would become a lifelong habit.

My singular moment of AOCS glory happened on the obstacle course one day. At one point on the course, we were tasked with jumping over a three-railed fence. The drill instructor shouted at me, "Bonnell! Go jump that fence!"

Having grown up on a farm, I'd jumped lots of fences. I ran up and, without breaking stride, put both hands on the top rail, swung my legs together over to the side, and cleared the fence. When I glanced back at our drill instructor, one side of his lip was raised in a smile. An actual smile. He shouted, "Now that's how you jump a fence! Bonnell! Do it again!"

I did stumble in one part of AOCS. Half of the class, including me, failed a navigation test, which meant we had to pack up our gear and drop back to join the class behind us. I'd "get to" enjoy my AOCS experience for an additional week. I took it in stride, hit the books, and passed the test the second time around.

★   ★   ★

The "survival training" element of AOCS was a weeklong battery of skill tests that took place near the end of the program, after we finished academics. First up, we were bused to an open area outside Pensacola, where we hiked in the sun for miles while learning to live off the land and navigate with a compass and chart.

We hadn't had any coffee for the first three months of AOCS— they didn't serve it in the chow hall—but someone caught a pygmy rattler and traded it to the SEAL leading our training in exchange for some. We brewed the grounds in a sock that I sacrificed for the cause. It probably wasn't the most sanitary way to brew coffee, but at least it was a sock I had never worn before.

The caffeine, on otherwise empty stomachs, was like a shot of adrenaline to our systems and kept us wound up that first night in the wilderness. We laughed and told funny AOCS stories until the sun came up. A couple of days later, we headed back to base hungry, sunburned, sleep-deprived, filthy, blistered, and covered in chigger bites, but we had crossed our first survival challenge off the list.

Next up was the Helo Dunker, a huge steel barrel with seating for six. The dunker simulates being inside of a helicopter during ditching, which is an emergency landing in water. We strapped into our seats in the dunker as it hung over a swimming pool; then the barrel was dropped into the water. Our job was to find our way out through one of the dunker's two exits. The second time we did the exercise, the barrel hit the water, then rolled upside down. We did it once more, this time wearing blacked-out goggles to simulate a nighttime environment. On that third round I was kicked in the face twice on the way out, and my goggles were knocked off. I had to repeat the exercise.

The following day we were introduced to the legendary Dilbert Dunker, which was designed to simulate another ditching event, this time in a jet rather than a helicopter. It was an interesting contraption beside yet another indoor swimming pool. It had a "cockpit" that was a roll cage built around an ejection seat. The whole thing was mounted on two rails that extended down into the pool. One candidate at a time, wearing flight gear and a helmet, was strapped into the Dilbert Dunker. When the operator pushed the release button, the cockpit slid down the rails, plunged into the pool, and flipped upside down. When the motion stopped, the candidate had to unstrap from the ejection seat and swim to the surface. An instructor was in the pool to make sure each candidate unclipped from the harness and swam out safely.

Honestly, this one didn't intimidate me. I had spent six summers as a lifeguard, taught swimming, and even done some synchronized swimming, so I was comfortable being underwater for long periods of time. When it was my turn, I was ready to go. An instructor buckled me in and checked to make sure the pool was clear. He gave the operator a thumbs-up, and the operator hit the release button. As I slid down the rails, I took a deep breath and braced for the impact. The cockpit hit the water, flipped upside down, and came to a stop. It was time to get to work. I quickly unclipped the two buckles, called Koch fittings, at my waist, then reached for the two at my shoulders. One released, but the other was stuck. I couldn't get the release bar to move.

What none of us realized was that a piece of nylon webbing from my torso harness was jammed in the buckle. This had happened when it was connected to the parachute in the ejection seat.

The instructor in the pool swam down to me and gave the buckle a couple of hard tugs, but no luck. He didn't have an air tank, so when he was out of air, he returned to the surface while I continued to hold my breath. A second diver appeared and yanked on the webbing and buckle unsuccessfully until he ran out of air as well; then he surfaced. I kept trying.

With most of the air inside my lungs expelled, I thought, *Are you kidding me? I have survived AOCS, passed every dang test!*

I'm a week away from graduating! A week away from earning my commission and heading to flight school! And now I am going to drown while doing the easy stuff? No! The answer is no! I am not dying today!

I yanked one last time with all my might and ripped the jammed webbing out of the Koch fitting. I lunged for the surface and came up on the back side of the machine. No one saw me. The entire class and both divers were on the other side of the dunker, yelling at the operator, "Pull it up! She's still down there! Pull it up!" They brought the dunker up, but I was gone. A hush came over the class; then they heard me gasping for breath while hanging on the other side of the pool. Unbelievably, the instructors made me strap back in and ride it again because they hadn't seen me get out of that contraption.

I made it through the rest of survival week—not necessarily unscathed, but unkilled.

The final week of AOCS was all that stood between me and my commission. During that week my classmates and I became candidate officers, which meant we served as the leaders for the next class starting the program. I left the "secure your luggage to the bulkhead" shouting to my peers and focused my attention on teaching the new class how to march—this time with jodies rather than college cheers.

On graduation day we donned our dress-white uniforms and were formally commissioned as officers in the United States Navy. After pinning on our ensign bars, we lined up to receive a salute and then a handshake from our drill instructor, whom we now outranked. Each newly minted ensign palmed a silver dollar and passed it off to the drill instructor in that handshake as a token of well-deserved respect.

I had cleared the first hurdle. I'd been tested and tried and had come out stronger, both physically and mentally. I didn't know it then, but habits were already forming in my life that would become invaluable instincts. Now it was time to face the next challenge, flight school.

CHAPTER 5

WOMAN IN A MAN'S WORLD

I've chased the shouting wind along, and flung
My eager craft through footless halls of air . . .
—JOHN GILLESPIE MAGEE JR., "HIGH FLIGHT"

On the long drive from Florida to Texas, reality began to set in: *I'm headed to flight training. Navy flight training!* It was June 1985, I was a commissioned officer in the Navy, and I had orders to report to Naval Air Station Corpus Christi for Primary Flight Training with squadron VT-27. I was both excited and a little anxious to tackle this next step. After all, as my mom had said so many years ago, "Those people are smart."

There were both Navy and Marine Corps pilots in the squadron, which was divided up into smaller groups called flights. I was one of the few Navy students in my flight, and I was the only woman in the entire squadron. The guys that I knew from AOCS were assigned to another flight, so I rarely saw them around the squadron.

I gathered that some of the Marines weren't altogether thrilled about my assignment to the same flight. They had just finished The Basic School (TBS) together, so they knew each other. And although I'm sure many of the men in my flight had gone to college with girls, there were few female Marines at that time and no female Marine aviators. I was an anomaly even within the Navy, the first branch of the US military to put women in jets. For the next two years, I would be the only woman in my squadrons. As I look back, I think this was a much bigger issue to others than it was to me.

Training started quickly with a few weeks of ground school—navigation, aerodynamics, and meteorology. We would be flying the Beechcraft T-34C Turbo Mentor, so we studied the aircraft's systems—hydraulics, fuel, electrical, and flight controls. All of this came before we ever set foot on the flight line.

My primary instructor, called an on-wing, was Captain Coston, a Marine Corps C-130 Hercules pilot and a perfect gentleman. Never once did he show a hint of dismay that he'd been assigned "the Navy girl." Initially he was one of few people in my flight who actually spoke to me.

When the time came, Captain Coston took me out under the blazing Texas sun and introduced me to the T-34. Compared to the Cessna 172 I had flown for a few hours back in New Mexico, the T-34 was a hot rod, a tandem-seat turbo prop with 550 horsepower.

When I was growing up, my mom had told me that girls don't sweat; they glow. On that first day I was glowing all over the ramp as I did the preflight inspection, but I didn't care. I was going flying! After the preflight I got a little ahead of myself. I practically jumped into the cockpit and strapped myself in. From the seat behind me I could hear Captain Coston laughing as he said, "Tammie Jo, look to your left. What do you see?" I'd left all of my flight gear lying on the ramp. I climbed out, grabbed my gear, put on my helmet and survival vest, and strapped myself back in. I'm sure this didn't go unnoticed and that those watching the Navy girl's first flight got a chuckle.

I worked through my checklists just like I had done dozens of times sitting in the "paper cockpit" (my apartment), then started the engine. It came to life with a whine, not a rumble, much smoother than the John Deere back on the ranch or even the piston engine in the Cessna. This was my first experience with a turbine engine.

The T-34 cockpit is set up like a Navy fighter, with the throttle on the left and the control stick in the middle, between the pilot's knees. Strapped to my right thigh was one of the most important parts of my flight gear—my kneeboard. It was a miniature desk with a clip to hold a notepad in place, a pencil on a lanyard, room for air traffic control frequencies, and even a light for reading notes in the dark. I'm a planner, and my kneeboard was full. I had written every word I should say to the air traffic controllers.

First, Clearance gave me my flight plan and my "squawk," the identification code that our aircraft would transmit. I talked to Ground next and received permission to taxi. Using the rudder pedals to steer, I navigated to the runway. *This is happening*, I thought. *It's really happening.*

My next communication was with Tower, who cleared me for takeoff and assigned me a heading and altitude to fly. I taxied around and found the runway centerline, then pushed up the throttle. Stepping on the right rudder to keep it straight, I headed down the runway. I watched my speed build, and when we hit 86 knots, I eased the stick back to raise the nose, and we were off! I even remembered to raise the landing gear.

From that point forward my assignment in Navy flight training often involved flying a specific altitude, airspeed, and heading. Later I would have much, much more to do, think about, and plan. Flying may look graceful from the ground, but for the pilot it's a constant "brain loop" of details that need to be kept in order—the best of puzzles and brain teasers put together. That day my mind was so busy with all of the details that I couldn't fully appreciate the wonder of the moment, not until later that night.

Captain Coston graded me on everything I did, from preflight to flying to headwork (decision-making), even to my attitude. I would be graded this way for the next two years. Every aspect of every student's every flight would be scrutinized by an instructor.

On that first flight, after I leveled off at three thousand feet, we headed to Waldron Field, an outlying practice airport away from the busy traffic pattern at NAS Corpus Christi. The first order of business in learning how to fly is learning how to land. At Waldron I would practice touch-and-goes. After touching down, instead of braking, I would add power and take off again without ever coming to a full stop.

Captain Coston directed me to turn left toward the coast, then turn again to parallel the shoreline. As we approached Wagon Wheel, the initial approach point for Waldron Field, he took the controls. To lose some altitude and enter the landing pattern, he rolled the plane upside down and did the second half of a barrel roll. He emerged from the maneuver perfectly at pattern altitude, lined up on the downwind in the landing pattern. That was the coolest thing I'd ever seen! He didn't explain the maneuver to me, but I took mental notes.

After demonstrating how to land the T-34, he handed over the controls and began talking me through the process. Heading, airspeed, altitude. Heading, airspeed, altitude. We went over the pattern again and again. Initially my landings weren't pretty, but Captain Coston didn't seem concerned. "Focus on flying a precise pattern, and the landings will come," he told me.

The next day Captain Coston and I retraced our route and flew over the same landmarks. Soon he said, "Okay, take me to Waldron Field." He left it up to me to find my way there and get into the landing pattern.

No problem, I thought. I followed the landmarks to Wagon Wheel and performed the same maneuver he'd done. I rolled the plane upside down and pulled the nose down toward the ground as I turned toward the field. My half barrel roll wasn't as pretty as his, but I did come out right side up and basically headed in the right direction. I was pretty proud of myself, but Captain Coston seemed caught off guard.

He yelled through the entire maneuver, and I didn't know why. "What in the world?! What are you doing?!" He was an even-tempered man, so I felt bad that I'd pushed him to this level of distress. I felt even worse about how that distress might spill over onto my grade sheet.

"Sir, I was entering the pattern like you showed me yesterday."

He remembered the aerobatic maneuver he had used the day before and started cracking up.

"I can see I'll have to be more careful about what I do in front of you," he said.

He had me depart the pattern and come back in again, this time in a more conventional way.

* ⋆ ⋆

Captain Coston never chastised me for my cowboy move, but he certainly teased me about it for the rest of my time in VT-27. Though he was friendly, it was a little tougher to get to know the other pilots in my flight. Primary Flight Training was intense, so everyone was busy, and as I've said, I was the only female aviator in sight. Each time I walked into the ready room, which is basically the pilots' breakroom, conversations stalled. As soon as I walked out, I could hear the chatter start up again. In the evenings after leaving the squadron, sometimes I would see a few guys I knew from AOCS. If we could afford to take a break from the books, we'd go for a run around the apartment complex. They'd laugh about the silly mistakes we all made in training and talk about their new friends in their flight. I was happy for them, but it drove home how alone I felt.

My parents had a phone at home by then, so I called my parents every day. One time I mentioned to my mom that I felt isolated. Everyone seemed to be developing friendships while I was stuck in solitary confinement. Ever practical, she said, "Invite them to your place for dinner. That's always a good way to make friends."

I protested. "Most of these guys are Marines just out of The Basic School. They're in warrior mode! They won't want to eat dinner with someone they don't even talk to around the squadron."

"Well, if you want a friend, be a friend," she said. I loved my sweet mom, but VT-27 wasn't sweet-mom country.

A couple of days later, as I approached the ready room, I heard Nelson Alberts, one of the biggest and loudest Marines, talking about a birthday package he'd received from his folks. As I walked in behind him, everyone went silent except for Nelson.

Realizing that someone was there, he slowly turned around to face me. Without missing a beat I said, "I'd be happy to make you a birthday dinner and cake. Why don't you invite four of your friends as well? It'll be fun."

He just stared at me.

I turned and walked out, shocked by my impulsiveness. *Oh my word! My mom just took over my body! Why did I say that?*

The next day, Nelson approached me and handed me a slip of paper with four names on it.

"Okay," he said. "Where do you live?"

At the appointed time, Nelson and four other Marines arrived at my door. They were lighthearted, happy to celebrate, and perfect gentlemen all evening. We talked and talked. No one explained why they hadn't talked to me earlier, but somehow it didn't matter anymore. The six of us became friends, and some of us studied together for the next two years.

★   ★   ★

Primary flight training isn't all about the airplanes. It's also about being introduced to the community and traditions of naval aviation.

As the new class, we were put in charge of the Solo Debrief. Every Friday afternoon after the flight line shut down, the squadron gathered at the Officers' Club for a beer and to listen to instructors roast the students who had done their first solo flight. Mainly it was an opportunity for pilots to get together after a long workweek and tell stories and drink a beer. The job of the new class was to set up and tear down.

At my first Solo Debrief, I was put in charge of setting up the beer table. This was a little funny because I'd never even tasted a beer. I hadn't grown up around alcohol at home, and MidAmerica Nazarene University was a dry campus. Nevertheless, I was happy to help out. I found a hundred cups, filled them with ice, then poured the beer. I'd always heard the guys talking about cold beer, so I was determined to make sure it was *cold*. Instead of appreciating my efforts, the squadron nearly court-martialed me over a hundred cups of watery beer.

The commanding officer bellowed, "All right, who's the wise guy?"

From then on, the running joke was that somebody had to serve as the Solo Debrief Beer Guard. *For heaven's sake, don't let Bonnell near the beer!*

My own first solo flight came a few weeks later, and it was epic! At least in my own mind. I felt like I was getting away with something. But before I could fly, I had work to do. I briefed my flight plan with Captain Coston, checked the weather, gathered up my flight gear, preflighted my trusty steed, and finally climbed into the cockpit—by myself. I worked through the same check-lists, followed the same procedures, and taxied out to the same runway. I was doing all of the things I had done with my instructor, but it felt completely different. More adventurous.

I'm going flying, and I'm the only one in this plane. When you're alone at the controls, you grow a little taller.

When I was in the air and at the practice area, I felt like someone had left the gate open and I'd gotten out. This was freedom! My oxygen mask did not seal well due to the grin I couldn't wipe off my face. I could do anything I wanted in my T-34. Of course, what I did was follow the flight plan I had briefed with Captain Coston, and I flew the maneuvers by the book. In truth, I was too nervous to do anything else. But I was solo! Surely this qualified me as a pilot, if only in my own mind.

Though my first solo flight couldn't have gone better, I was sweating the Solo Debrief. Yes, the instructor gives a little speech that roasts his student, but the student gets a turn to do the same. Everybody votes on whose speech is best, and the vote always goes to the instructor. I wasn't concerned about that so much as what traditionally follows: the student unzips his flight suit, and his instructor cuts off the student's T-shirt. I lost sleep over what to do about this. While I didn't want to draw attention to myself by dodging a tradition, I was certain about one thing: I would *not* have any clothing cut off of me in public.

That Friday I walked into the Officers' Club wearing two T-shirts, dreading the shirt cutting but prepared for the roast. A witty fellow student had helped me write a funny but factual poem about Captain Coston, and it was more successful than I could have hoped. When the votes were tallied, we were all surprised that my roast won. Ever the gentleman, Captain Coston laughed, handed me the scissors, and offered his own back to me so I could cut off *his* shirt.

My next challenge in Primary Flight Training was learning how to fly instruments—that is, with no outside visual cues, just the instruments in the cockpit. Tom, a friend in the class ahead of me, became a great study partner. Before my instrument checkride he gave me some chocolate, a set of Navy gold wings, and a card bearing the words from Luke 18:27: "The things that are impossible with people are possible with God." That was just the encouragement I needed, and I ended up doing fine on the instrument checkride.

Over the next few months I worked my way through the rest of the syllabus and learned navigation, formation (flying together with other aircraft), and aerobatics.

At the end of Primary, students are assigned to one of three training "pipelines": jets, props (propeller aircraft), or helos (helicopters). Each week of Primary, students are ranked according to their grades. That class ranking, a student's preferences, and the overriding "needs of the Navy" determine which pipeline each student enters. I'd done well in the program, made the Commodore's List (which is like an honor roll), and finished second in my class. When the orders were handed out, I got my first choice: jets!

By the time I finished Primary, I had forgotten I was the only woman. I'd enjoyed my time in the squadron and the friendships I formed there. The instructors gave me a hard time in a friendly way and wished me well. My friend Nelson presented me with Marine dog tags and declared me an honorary Marine. That gesture still makes me smile. My given Marine name is Tammie Jo Billy Bob Bonnell, United States Marine Corps. I accepted the dog tags but refused to answer to such a mouthful of nonsense.

I couldn't have hoped for a better beginning.

*   *   *

From Corpus Christi the Navy sent me to VT-26, an Intermediate Jet Training squadron at NAS Beeville, Texas (also called Chase Field), to learn how to fly the mighty T-2 Buckeye. The T-2 was never considered the sleekest jet in the military's lineup. The plump-bodied Buckeye had straight wings with tip tanks and dual engines along the belly of the fuselage. Due to its shape, it was affectionately referred to as the Guppy. But the T-2 had its virtues, one of which was it was built like a tank, just perfect for taking the pounding of aircraft-carrier landings.

Hotel-room-style housing—the Bachelor Officers Quarters (BOQ)—was available to singles on base in Beeville, but I found a big house out in the country instead, about sixteen miles away from base. It felt more like home to me although, to pay the rent, I'd need to find two roommates. Again, I was the only woman in my squadron, but two of the guys in my class wanted to live off base as well. This was definitely unconventional in my mind, but my straitlaced parents were supportive, so the guys and I signed the lease. I took the upstairs, and they took the downstairs.

That arrangement lasted a week. The guys realized the oven wasn't going to be turned on unless they did it, so they needed to be closer to fast food. I'm glad to say that wasn't the end of our friendship, only our living arrangement. The homeowner graciously let me pay a third of the rent until I found new roommates, which didn't take long. Two young ladies from my church, high school teachers, soon joined me.

The squadron at Beeville was quick to welcome me. Commander Fred Grant was an admirable skipper, and his instructors were friendly. I was soon invited to be on the squadron's softball team. They even let me play. When I was paired with an on-wing whose call sign was Clyde, the other instructors thought it was hilarious to write my last name, Bonnell, on the schedule as "Bonnie." I wound up keeping this call sign throughout my Navy career.

The Navy seems to always be plagued with either a shortage or a glut of pilots. At the time I was going through VT-26, there was a shortage, so the pressure was on to progress quickly. My classmates and I typically flew twice a day, which was fine with me. Other than church on Sunday and a softball game or two during the week, I buried myself in the books and could not have been happier.

Some of the phases of T-2 training were repeats of the T-34, only performed at much higher speeds. We had aircraft familiarization flights and practiced flying and navigating with instruments. One of my favorite phases of flight training was formation flying. It seemed to come naturally to me, and I caught on quickly to the rhythm of flying in close proximity to other aircraft. In the T-34, we had learned to fly in a "section" of two aircraft. Now, in jets, we would be flying in four-ship "divisions." I couldn't wait.

Things were going well until I was assigned to fly with Captain Cornejo, an exchange pilot from Venezuela. He had been a member of Venezuela's flight demonstration team, so he lived and breathed formation flying. Unfortunately he didn't even try to hide the fact that he considered it an insult to be assigned a female student. On our first flight together he came out to the plane while I was doing the preflight check. He was steaming.

"Women don't fly!" he said to me. "There's a reason they don't fly!"

I gave him my attention but didn't respond.

"I tell them, I do not fly with female!" Then, as I kicked my foot up in the aircraft's first step, he asked me, "Do you cry?"

"Not in the cockpit," I said as I climbed into the jet.

He followed suit, mounting the kicksteps as if he might put his boots right through the plane, then dropped into the back seat, still grumbling. Most of it was in Spanish, which was best for me. Since I didn't speak the language well enough to understand it, his grumbling was easier to ignore.

To his credit, Captain Cornejo was open to a change of heart, and change he did. I had a great formation flight, which apparently impressed him. By the time we taxied in and shut the aircraft down, I had won him over. He even went to the scheduling office and requested to be my formation instructor for the duration of the program.

The flight-training syllabus takes a building-block approach.

The block after formation flying was air-to-air gunnery. In that phase we would go out as a four-ship formation to the operating area and set up a circular pattern around a banner being towed by another T-2. The purpose was to learn how to roll in off of a high perch and maneuver into position to shoot down another aircraft. To have four aircraft simultaneously flying this pattern required a precisely choreographed dance. It was incredibly dynamic and absolutely fun.

Most phases of training involved multiple flights, but there was one phase that consisted of a single sortie: the OCF, or out-of-control flight. All students had to demonstrate that they could recover the aircraft from an out-of-control situation, either a stall or a spin, before they were allowed to fly solo. The only way to do that was to climb up to altitude and depart controlled flight in a variety of ways, over and over and over again.

My OCF wasn't particularly frightening to me, but it was definitely unlike any other flying experience I'd had. I guess I took my cue from my instructor, who seemed relaxed in the brief. Seated behind me, he flew the Buckeye to almost thirty thousand feet, pulled the throttles back to idle, and held the nose on the horizon. The airspeed needle rolled back, the plane stalled, and the nose dropped below the horizon, just as he had told me it would. Then he gave the controls to me to recover. I relaxed pressure on the stick and eased it forward, which allowed the aircraft to "seek flight," and reentered controlled flight again. That wasn't bad at all!

My instructor took us back to altitude, and we progressed from simple power-off stalls to "rudder triplets," in which the aircraft was pointed straight up at zero airspeed and the rudders were kicked in to cause a spin. He departed flight in different ways each time, then gave the controls to me to recover.

Up and down and around and around we went for about an hour. The syllabus required about ten different departures from flight. When I had checked all of the blocks and my instructor was satisfied that I could handle an out-of-control aircraft, I headed back to base and landed, my OCF complete.

★　★　★

Intermediate jet training in the Buckeye culminated with what sets Navy jet pilots apart from the rest: aircraft-carrier landings. Landing an aircraft on a ship is, without question, one of the most challenging tasks required of a naval aviator. Staff Sergeant Carney's insistence on attention to detail, which he'd drilled into our heads from day one of AOCS, came to mean something real. To safely land a jet on a ship, a thousand details have to come together, and fudging even one of those details can kill you or someone else. This phase of training would stand out as a unique challenge that forged a new set of nerves in me.

Our initial practice took place on a nice, stable runway painted to look like a carrier deck. Beside the runway was what we called the "meatball," a light system that lets pilots know if they're on the proper glide slope. Landing Signal Officers (LSOs) stood beside the runway and talked to us on the radio as we flew our approaches, just like they would on the aircraft carrier. We did Field Carrier Landing Practice (FCLP) twice a day for a few weeks. We would take off, turn directly into the landing pattern, and do touch-and-goes until we were out of gas. We made hundreds of passes.

In Primary Flight Training, Captain Coston had taught me the "heading, airspeed, altitude" scan. For carrier landings, pilots learned a more advanced three-point scan, which we would repeat from the moment we rolled into the groove to the moment our air-craft's wheels hit the deck: meatball (glide slope), lineup (with the centerline on the runway), and angle of attack (another term for airspeed). Over and over and over again: meatball, lineup, angle of attack. Always checking and correcting and never settling for less than perfection.

There was no carrier landing simulator for the T-2, so the first time a Buckeye pilot got a picture of what an aircraft carrier looked like was from behind, when flying out to land on it—solo. The joke was you couldn't *pay* anyone enough to sit in the back seat the first time a pilot had to "go to the boat." The real reason was the student needed to be 100 percent focused on the task at hand, not worrying about what an instructor in the back seat was thinking. For this qualification, the instructor was the LSO watching and talking to you over the radio from the flight deck.

A runway on the ground is a fixed constant; an aircraft car-rier is anything but. With each swell of the ocean, the deck of the carrier rises and falls. It rolls from side to side and front to back. It's an ever-moving target—and a small one. My first good look at USS *Lexington*—or any aircraft carrier, for that matter—was from several thousand feet overhead. It looked tiny. At that moment I understood why naval aviators always referred to the carrier as "the boat." An aircraft carrier in port is massive. It is a *ship*. When it's at sea and you're going to land on it, it's a postage stamp.

The *Lexington* was almost three football fields in length and more than 147 feet wide. The flight deck was basically divided into two sections. The front half, from the island to the bow, had two catapults for launching aircraft. The back half consisted of a landing area that angled off slightly to the left. This design allowed for simultaneous launch and recovery operations. I could plainly see the small angled deck with the four "wires" (cables) strung across it. I was just having a hard time believing I was about to land on it.

My flight, a lead plus three other students, circled over the "Lady Lex" in what is called the marshal stack while we waited our turn behind another flight of T-2s. Off to the starboard (right) side of the ship, a helicopter was in a loose holding pattern in case a pilot ejected and needed to be fished out of the water. I was trying to stay in formation as well as take all of this in when the air boss called our flight's number.

Even with all that practice, I didn't know when my heart had ever beat so fast. After our flight lead took us out of the stack and maneuvered down toward the carrier, he led us into the break over the ship. When it was my turn, I would break hard left and pull my throttles to idle. I'd pull about five g's to bleed off my speed from 350 knots down to about 130, roll out after 180 degrees of turn on downwind (heading in the opposite direction from the ship), and put my landing gear and flaps down. Then I'd put my hook down to make my first "trap," or arrested landing on a carrier. The hook hung below the back of the aircraft and was designed to catch a cable wire and stop the jet.

I came into the break at eight hundred feet above the water, held that through the break turn, then descended to six hundred feet on downwind until it was time to start the descending turn. If I did this right, I'd come out right on glide slope when I rolled out of the turn behind the boat.

Each aircraft was spaced about one minute behind the aircraft ahead. This allowed the deck crew just enough time to disengage an aircraft from the arresting cable after a trap and to get the cable reset while the aircraft taxied out of the landing area. It was poetry in motion in one of the most dangerous work environments in the world.

About halfway through my approach turn, I started to pick up the meatball out the left side of my canopy. It was slightly high and settling into the center as I came around the corner, which meant I was right on glide slope. As I rolled into the groove, the LSO said over the radio, "One twenty-six, call the ball."

"One twenty-six, Buckeye ball, six-point-two," I said, indicating my call sign, aircraft type, and fuel state. Knowing the fuel state of every aircraft operating around the carrier was critical, particularly in a training environment. They never wanted an aircraft around the ship that didn't have enough gas to get back to shore.

The boat's movement through water generates wind over the deck, so the centerline of the angle deck was always moving slowly to the right. If the LSOs saw a pilot deviating too much from centerline, they would make a call, either "Right for lineup" or "Come left." If a pilot got low or high on glide slope, the LSOs would make a "Power" or "You're high" call. Frankly, I don't remember what calls they made to me, but I do remember thinking that as foreign as this was, it was also familiar: meatball, lineup, angle of attack; meatball, lineup, angle of attack; always correcting, all the way to impact.

WHAM!

I landed with a jolt, and the next thing I knew, I was hanging in the straps as I came to an abrupt stop. On touchdown I had shoved the throttles full forward so that, had I not caught a wire, I would have been powered up and ready to fly again.

A carrier pilot always has to be ready for things that could go wrong. Once during my training, a pilot who landed after me caught a wire but wasn't lined up properly and went over the edge. There's a catwalk around the edge of the carrier and, in some areas, netting that can catch people should they misstep or get jet blasted, but neither one is designed to catch a T-2. Because the pilot's tailhook had caught a wire, it held him in a precarious position, hanging over the edge of the carrier, until crews could bring out the crane to haul him up onto the deck.

On that first attempt of mine, I had lined up properly and caught a wire. I had my first trap! As much as I wanted to savor the moment, there was no time for that. A yellow shirt (taxi director) gave me the signal to throttle back to idle and keep my feet off the brakes. I felt a tug backward as they retracted the arresting cable. The yellow shirt gave me the signal to raise my hook and start taxiing with a hard-right turn. The first order of business was to get across the line designating the edge of the landing area. One of my classmates was rolling into the groove right behind me, and I needed to be out of his way.

I cleared the landing area and was passed off to another yellow shirt, who gave me taxi directions toward the bow of the ship. My first carrier landing was a success, but the celebration would have to wait.

Next up was my first catapult launch. To prep for this "cat shot," I followed the taxi directions, which lined me up with one of the *Lexington*'s two catapults. When directed, I lowered the launch bar on the nose gear of my jet, and the catapult crew secured the plane into the catapult's shuttle. They raised the blast deflector behind the plane as I confirmed my aircraft's weight with the crew.

I was directed to push my throttles up to full power—I could feel the jet squat as it went into tension. I gave the shooter (the officer in charge of operating the catapults) a sharp salute, signaling that I was ready to go. He looked down the catapult track one more time to ensure that it was safe to launch me, returned my salute, and pushed a button that sent me on an E-ticket ride.

I accelerated from zero to about 150 miles an hour in two and a half seconds, and it felt like someone had kicked me in the backside. Legend has it that the *Lexington*'s catapults can sling a Volkswagen bug more than a mile. I don't know if that's true, but I'm inclined to believe it.

The deck of an aircraft carrier sits about sixty feet above the water, and the cat shot sends a jet straight off the bow of the ship. We'd been warned not to climb out after the launch too quickly at that airspeed because, at that altitude, there would be no chance of recovery if a pilot raised the nose too fast and stalled. Besides, the instructors teased, "It makes you look like you're afraid of the water." The last thing I wanted was to look like a sissy, so I overcompensated a bit.

After the cat shot I kept flying straight ahead about sixty feet off the surface . . . for a while. The feeling of being launched was so intense, I guess I was lost in the moment, enjoying the ride. My instructor took note of my low flight. Afterward he jokingly scribbled in my logbook: "Check for mackerel in the intakes."

It was May 1986, and the movie *Top Gun* had just been released. After we returned from our first trip to the carrier, our commanding officer rented the entire theater in Beeville for all of the students and instructors in the squadron to see the film. I loved it! It captured the emotion of carrier aviation, the dynamics of catapult launches and traps, and the rush of raw adrenaline that naval aviators experience. Over the next few years I would get "carrier qualified" in the A-4, then go back as a T-2 instructor. Each time on the carrier was an incredible rush—for me, but not for my parents.

"Don't tell us when you're going to the boat," they eventually told me. "We only want to know when you get back."

Career-wise, I was on a high. I was carrier qualified and on my way to Advanced Jet Training. Finishing second in my class again gave me a boost of confidence that I did have what it takes to become a naval aviator. I had no idea I was about to meet a pilot determined to keep that from happening.

CHAPTER 6

DOGFIGHTS

Peace is not the absence of conflict, but the
ability to cope with conflict by peaceful means.
—RONALD REAGAN

In those days, before smartphones put the world in the palms of our hands, we took more time to notice the real world around us. Sometimes, if an image was truly profound, it stuck with you. I still recall one of those mental snapshots. As I drove to base one evening from my house in the country, I saw an A-4 take off. It was silhouetted in front of a big yellow moon that was rising right up over the road. Time seemed to stand still for a moment, and I remember thinking, *I'm getting ready to do that!*

The Douglas A-4 Skyhawk was a jet you simply couldn't fly without feeling really cool. The A-4 was a true combat jet. It was the Navy's carrier-based light-attack aircraft for the early years of the Vietnam War, and it was flown for a few years by the Blue Angels, the Navy's flight demonstration team. It was a serious delta-winged fighter, not a straight-winged trainer. Straight wings are much stabler and more forgiving to fly, harder to stall, and easier to recover from mistakes. Delta-wing aircraft are the opposite, but what they lose in stability, they gain in maneuverability. The Skyhawk seemed to silently say, "Sissies need not apply."

I stayed in Beeville for Advanced Jet Training and was assigned to a squadron right across the street, VT-25. It had been nicknamed the Nazi Squadron and was proud of its reputation. Many of my friends from Intermediate training had gone to the other Advanced squadron, VT-24, which was known as the Happy Batt (*Batt* being short for *Battalion*). They did seem to have a better time, but VT-25 would serve as a proving ground for my resolve to become a naval aviator.

As in Primary and Intermediate training, we went to ground school first, then tackled instrument simulators. Our first taste of the real jet was a continuation of instrument training, starting with a few local flights, then an instrument cross-country, which usually took place over a weekend. Cross-country flights were like road trips. They were an opportunity to practice flight planning, flying by instruments, and shooting approaches to unfamiliar airports. An added bonus was the chance to get out of Beeville—and in an A-4, you could get away in a hurry.

Typically, the cross-country flight was planned by the on-wing instructor and his student together. There would be some give-and-take about where they would fly for the weekend. Maybe they'd go out to NAS Miramar in San Diego, home of the Navy Fighter Weapons School (TOPGUN) and the West Coast–based F-14 Tomcat squadrons. Or maybe they'd go to the student's hometown to show mom and dad the new jet. While a cross-country trip was serious training, it could also be some serious fun.

As the time for my cross-country approached, however, I was surprised to get a summons to the operations officer's office.

The Ops O, as we called him, held a powerful position in the squadron—third in the chain of command behind the commanding officer (CO) and the executive officer (XO). I was more than a little nervous about why I'd been singled out of my class to report to his office. I'd never met him, and when I arrived, he didn't introduce himself. He simply informed me that he would be my instructor for my instrument cross-country, then handed me a sheet of paper with the information I needed to plan the trip and get the required authorizations. The meeting was a one-way conversation, and then it was over. Not sure how to respond, I said, "Yes, sir," and left the office.

Later, when I mentioned to a few of my friends in the squadron that I was going on my cross-country with the Ops O, they were horrified. Apparently, he had a well-established reputation as a womanizer who hit on female students. Rumor had it that those who didn't acquiesce risked a failing grade.

I was shocked. This couldn't be happening. The only thing I could think was, *I'm taller than he is. I'm sure he's not attracted to me.*

As the day approached, and I could see no way out of flying with this predator, my mind raced with ideas about how to avoid his traps. I have to admit I was praying hard that he would get sick.

Miraculously, on the Friday we were scheduled to leave, I was the one who got sick. I woke up with a wretched sinus infection. Not just a case of the sniffles, but a full-blown fever and head of woe. I'd never been so happy to feel so miserable! When my cross-country was rescheduled, it was with my on-wing rather than the Ops O. Word around the squadron was that the Ops O wasn't happy. I knew I'd dodged a bullet, but I was also pretty sure I hadn't heard the last from him.

* * *

I had about ten flights in the A-4 when an enlisted para rigger pulled me aside one morning in the paraloft, where we stored our flight gear. In a discreet voice he said, "If you need to get a custom torso harness made, there's a place out in China Lake where you can get it done." I shrugged, not knowing why he was telling me this. China Lake was all the way out in California, and my torso harness, while not a perfect fit, got the job done. He repeated himself like it was some big secret: "*China Lake.*"

The entire exchange was bizarre. I had heard of pilots who, for whatever reason, needed a custom torso harness, but I didn't think I was one of them. Even if I was, I really didn't get why the information would be communicated as a secret.

A few days later it all made sense. That morning the ready room was full of instructors and students when the Ops O walked in, stood about ten feet away from me, and loudly announced, "Bonnell, you're going to have to check out of the jet pipeline and go fly props."

The place fell silent, and I felt like the world was staring at me. He was kicking me out of the program!

"Sir?" I asked, hoping for an explanation.

"Your torso harness doesn't fit," he explained. "We can't

have you flying around in something that might injure you if you eject." He spoke like it was a done deal. I was out, and that was all there was to it.

I was stunned for a moment before the hushed advice of the para rigger came back to me. I said, "Sir, I was told the guys who need a custom-fit harness just go out to China Lake and have one made in a day."

The Ops O didn't respond. He simply turned and walked out. I glanced around and caught the sympathetic eyes of a few of my friends, who were shaking their heads in disbelief. It was obvious to everyone in the room that I had a target on me. I was just grateful that someone (thank you, para riggers) had seen what was coming and warned me.

I went to California, had the harness made, and that was the last I heard of it. While it was clearly not his intent, the Ops O had actually done me a favor. The new custom harness fit much better than my old one. I wrote in my journal, "I am amazed at how God orchestrated the snippet of conversation that saved my jet career."

After the sinus infection that rescued me from a cross-country with the Ops O, I had a running battle with colds that I couldn't seem to kick. But I wasn't about to let a little congestion keep me off the flight schedule. The A-4 syllabus was intense, and every flight was more dynamic, and more fun, than the last.

During one night flight, I went out with a stuffy nose. Suddenly I felt as if someone had shoved an ice pick through my head. The pain was excruciating for a moment, but it eased up and improved once I was back on the ground. I pressed on, but after more painful flights I knew I was getting worse and would have to see the flight surgeon.

My diagnosis was not good. Flying congested, I'd blown an

upper sinus; then that sinus had also become infected. Now the infection was entrenched. The flight surgeon grounded me until it cleared up.

Normally a pilot in my condition was allowed bed rest, which is what the doctor initially recommended, but the Ops O had different plans for me. He shrugged when I turned in my med-down chit (the doctor's memo) and ordered me to desk duty until I was better. I had to man the squadron duty desk for a twelve-hour shift every other night, from 8:00 p.m. to 8:00 a.m.

While on duty I was supposed to be alert and ready because I was the point of contact should any squadron personnel or aircraft have an emergency. That first night I was anything but alert and ready. I was nauseated, and my head was pounding. All I wanted to do was curl up and sleep. A night stretched into a week. Then a week turned into a month. Then one month became two. I simply could not get better.

My journals during that stretch of life reflect that I was down. Not just med down but depressed. I felt like I was being left behind as I watched my class, and even classes behind mine, move on through the program. I had to remind myself I was more than what I did. I had worth in God's eyes regardless of whether I was med up or med down, whether I pleased the Ops O or not, even whether I was a naval aviator or not. At one point I wrote, "Lord, I fear I'm forgetting much and forgetting my battle to be who I am without apology for being a woman. You made me and I know there is a reason you made me a girl."

Even then I knew that what I've been given is sacred—from the color of my eyes to my gender to my faith to my love of flying. Everything that makes me who I am is a gift, and I need to treat it that way. I'm sure everyone fights to discover and hold on to their identity as they navigate the working world. Military flight training isn't the only high-pressured profession that brings on such stress and tests—it was just the one I was pursuing.

Two months turned into three. Finally, mercifully, my blown sinus healed. I was able to pick up where I'd left off despite being pretty rusty and a few months behind schedule. All of my friends in the program had finished and pinned on their wings of gold. They were full-fledged naval aviators, off learning how to fly their assigned fleet aircraft, while I was still back in Beeville surrounded by students I didn't know. No doubt I was down, but I was nowhere near out.

★   ★   ★

During my time in VT-25, it seemed there was always a challenge before me—not the good challenges of conquering the Navy flight program but daily struggles to defend my right to be in it. This struggle created a battle within me. I was constantly weighing whether I should dig a hole and hide or build a fort and fight. How could I avoid living constantly on the defensive? My focus on flight training was all too often distracted by the need to calculate my next move in the chess match I played to survive. But one move was never on the table: quitting. The naysayers would have to kick me out if they were going to get rid of me.

Instead of squeezing a stress ball, I kept writing in my journal. I addressed a number of entries to someone of high enough rank to make a difference. This habit saved me from having to carry offenses around with me. Unloading them on the page helped me resist the temptation to unload on friends at the squadron. Not only did this lighten my mental load; it also helped me to remember that I wasn't facing life alone. I knew God had my back.

As I wrote about my trials, it also became clear to me that

I was being opposed by individuals, *not* an organization. Some unscrupulous people abused their authority and wielded their personal beliefs as weapons, but they didn't represent the whole. The Navy wanted me in the program, even if there were those within the Navy who didn't.

Conversely, journaling reminded me that God had also put plenty of good-hearted people in my path. Once, the wife of an instructor gave me a small present: a hand-stitched Christmas ornament with the squadron's logo on it. She handed it to me privately at a party and whispered, "I made this for you. Keep going! My husband has told me how they sometimes treat you, and we're both sorry." I was especially touched because, although I knew of her husband, we had never flown together. The ornament still hangs on my family's Christmas tree every year.

*   *   *

When you're an underdog, it's easy to look at life through the lens of victimhood, but that perspective can distort the truth. Sometimes trials are just trials, as I experienced during formation, one of my favorite phases of flight training.

Formation flying starts with a rendezvous, also known as a join-up. If you're going to fly together, you have to get together, and there's a proper way to do it.

During one formation flight, poor weather at the airfield required me to have a safety observer in my back seat. The instructor in the lead aircraft, a Marine I knew from church, was in charge of the flight. My safety observer and I broke through the low cloud layer to a beautifully sunny sky and headed to the rendezvous point. I spotted the flight lead and fell into position below and behind him.

A rendezvous is part science and part art, and I like both. Geometry says that if you're flying a tighter circle than the lead aircraft and gradually increase the size of your circle while maintaining a constant bearing, the circles will merge, and you'll join up. The art is in accomplishing that quickly and smoothly with subtle stick and throttle movements. Captain Cornejo, my T-2 formation savant from Venezuela, had taught me well. I wasted no time that day as I slid up the bearing line of my flight lead's A-4. I arrived in position off his left side and in one fluid motion slid under his jet and took position just off his right wing. It was probably my most expeditious rendezvous ever, and the safety observer, who was also an instructor, was going crazy in the back seat.

"That was awesome! Smoking hot! Best I've seen!" he shouted over the intercom. That was certainly nice to hear and a great way to start the flight.

After landing and shedding my flight gear, I headed to the debrief. On my way I overheard my back seater bragging on me. It was so refreshing to hear praise. I was on cloud nine. But when I arrived in the briefing room, the flight lead said, "Bonnell, that was a dangerous join-up, and I'm giving you a down for it."

I was stunned. A down was a failing grade, and I'd never had one in all of my flight training. I wished my safety observer was in the debrief, but he wasn't grading me that day. I tried to wrap my mind around how two instructors could have such different perspectives on the same flight.

To make sense of this, my mind circled back to science and art. Science is objective and concrete. Two plus two always equals four. Art, on the other hand, is subjective. Beauty is in the eye of the beholder. One instructor loved the way I had painted that rendezvous, and the other wasn't impressed. In the end I had to let it go and not waste time worrying about whether I'd been graded fairly. What was not subject to opinion was that I had to do the flight over. When I did, I slowed my rendezvous down to what felt like a snail's pace, passed the exercise, and pressed on.

Next up was air-to-ground weapons training. There were no bombing ranges around Beeville, Texas, so we went on a weapons detachment to NAF El Centro, California. Apart from some irrigated farmland, El Centro is surrounded by desolate desert. With miles and miles of nothing but dirt and rocks, it's the perfect place to practice dropping bombs. The base also serves as the winter training grounds for the Blue Angels.

This would be my first time to drop bombs and strafe (shoot the gun mounted in the aircraft). As much as I had loved to shoot when growing up, I couldn't wait. This was going to take target practice to a whole new level! The A-4 made me think of a quarter horse that needed a worthy mission to be truly happy, and putting bombs on target was definitely a worthy mission for the A-4. It was what it was made for. This would prove to be my favorite part of Advanced Jet Training, and it would also hold one of my fondest memories from flight school.

One of the responsibilities of the flight lead was to keep the operation on schedule, and our weapons detachment motto was "On target, on time." Students took turns briefing and leading flights, and when it was my turn, I conducted a thorough but expeditious brief covering all of the admin, tactical, and safety aspects of our high-angle bombing sortie. I wrapped up the brief a little ahead of schedule, put on my gear, and headed out to my plane.

I noticed that I was alone as I walked out to my jet. The other pilots were suited up, but they hung back, talking with each other by the hangar-bay doors. I climbed up and put my helmet bag in the cockpit, checked that the master arm switch was in the

SAFE position, and headed back down to begin my preflight. I still didn't see the other pilots and started grumbling to myself, "I will be on target, on time, even if I'm solo!" That famous *Top Gun* quote, "I will not leave my wingman," didn't apply to those who didn't get it in gear and start their engines.

I was reaching for one of the twenty-five-pound practice bombs to give it a shake when I recoiled in shock. My bombs were dripping in *pink paint!* That was their cue. The other pilots finally came out of the hangar bay. Together with the ground crew, they were howling. I guess you could say they were tickled pink with themselves. I admit I laughed inside, remembering from grade school that kids only tease kids they like.

While that was all fun, we had a mission to do, and I was not going to let my flight get behind. After preflight and startup we all taxied out, but the Blue Angels called for taxi about the same time, and when the Blues move, everything else stops. We waited at the hold-short on the taxiway at the takeoff end of the runway. As the Blues taxied by my A-4, one of them keyed the mic and announced on Tower frequency, "Nice bombs!" Since I had my helmet on, I doubt he realized I was a girl and that pink didn't bother me. I put those pink bombs on target . . . on time.

*   *   *

As a child, I had watched the T-38s dogfight in the skies over my family's ranch. Now it was my turn. Aerial Combat Maneuvering (ACM), or dogfighting, followed weapons training. And it was, hands down, the most dynamic flying I had ever done. As in weapons training, the object was to destroy a target, but in ACM the target was another aircraft coming at you with one thousand miles an hour of closure.

Basic ACM starts with two aircraft flying parallel to each other but a few miles apart. At the "Fight's on" call, they turn in and fly toward each other until they hit the merge, or pass. At that point it becomes a high-speed, three-dimensional, twisting, turning match with each pilot jockeying for position behind the other. If a pilot is able to "saddle up" behind his opponent and get the aircraft's gunsight on the other jet, the call over the radio is "Guns!" It's a call you always want to make and never want to hear. These engagements don't usually last long and often end in a draw when either jet hits the "hard deck," which is an altitude of ten thousand feet above the ground.

When I went med down earlier in the program and was separated from my class, the timing was such that I didn't fit neatly into another class. By the time I reached ACM, the only other student in the same phase was a friend of mine, Bill Calvert. Since we were the only two pilots, we were opponents in the air. Bill was more than happy to study together on the ground so we both would be better fighters, a true testimony to his character. He and his wife, Lori, often invited me over to their home for dinner. Bill and I would talk through the next flight in the syllabus, and when we thought we were ready, Lori would quiz us.

Bill's gunsight spent a fair amount of time on my jet. But on one particular engagement that stands out in my memory, I did get to roll in behind him.

We had done our head-on pass and pulled up, jockeying for position behind each other. We flew up into the sun, then came down again, a tactical move that causes your opponent to lose sight of you. About halfway through the engagement, Bill and I were tangled up in a flat scissors. We had our noses parked high in the air, flying as slowly as possible without stalling as we weaved back and forth, each trying to get behind the other. I thought I had enough space to turn in behind him, but I misjudged. I had to think fast because I was shooting out in front of him. I dipped the plane's nose a little more, gained a bit more airspeed, then did a barrel roll over him. This move caused me to lose airspeed—just the amount I needed to come up right behind him. My instructor let out a whoop and said, "Guns!" Bill, always gracious, had a chuckle at my "save."

During the last few ACM flights in the program, the weather turned foggy, so again I was required to have a safety observer riding in the back seat. I didn't mind—until I learned it would be the Ops O who had given me so much grief, from my first cross-country flight to the torso-harness fiasco to the night-duty assignment when I should have been on bed rest.

If you have ever dealt with negative thoughts that will not stop inserting themselves into your normally happy world, that was what it was like having the Ops O in my back seat. Though he was strictly there as a safety precaution and was supposed to only observe, he did his best to purposefully distract me and denigrate my every move—even my anticipated moves. I'm all for constructive criticism, but I don't think he had a constructive bone in his body. His presence tested my ability to separate what he was saying from what I needed to do.

I came to think of him as a coral snake. He wasn't noble enough to give a warning rattle before striking, and he had no fangs. He would just chew on a person until he could break the skin and introduce his venom. If I could have, I'd have put him in a Coke bottle, something that took the sass out of snakes we caught when I was growing up.

On our first flight together, he informed me that I didn't have the sleeves of my flight suit folded the way he liked them. Because he outranked my instructor, he assumed the right to grade me, then gave me a "below average" for my sleeves, even though there is no standard for this. He dinged me because he could.

The next day he screamed a few times for no other reason than to be distracting. Then he gave me another below-average mark because my voice was "too high."

After that flight I did something I'd never done before. I went to talk to the scheduler and asked for a reprieve. I noticed on the scheduler's board that the Ops O wasn't scheduled as a back seater with anyone else. I asked if I could have a different back seater the next day.

The scheduling officer, a Marine, apologetically said yes. He told me they never put the Ops O in anyone's back seat because he was such "a screamer." He told me the Ops O had been coming in, removing my assigned observer, and penciling in himself instead. I could only assume it was to take a few last shots at my GPA.

Fortunately Marines have a way of getting things done. Even though the Ops O outranked him, somehow the scheduler was able to put an end to my back-seat screamer.

In spite of the Ops O's efforts, I finished near the top of my class and with a high enough GPA to qualify to be a Selectively Retained Graduate (SERGRAD), a pilot with wings and an invitation to teach in one of the training squadrons. My last flight ended with a splash; it was the squadron's tradition to dump a bucket of ice water over the heads of students who finished the program. Some of my girlfriends came out to celebrate with us, and we took a chick pic. I noticed we all wore something pink—unplanned but wonderfully girlish.

It was also a tradition for squadron leaders who were available to come out on the ramp for the last-flight celebration. I don't know if the Ops O was there or not. It didn't matter anymore. I couldn't help but feel I had won that battle.

★   ★   ★

My next orders sent me back across the street to VT-26, the T-2 squadron. Commander Fred Grant had requested that I come back as one of his SERGRADs. I considered this an honor and said yes. It felt like a golden ticket to me. He was an outstanding leader, and by then I had seen firsthand how leadership sets the tone, positive or negative. There was no one I would have rather worked for. An added bonus was that after a two-year SERGRAD tour, I would have a better chance of getting my first choice for my next aircraft assignment.

My first year as a T-2 instructor passed without a hitch. I enjoyed teaching new students and loved the camaraderie of the squadron. Life was good. After paying my dues for a year as a new instructor teaching the basics of flying jets, it was my turn to get my advanced qualifications and start teaching gunnery and carrier landings.

Unfortunately a change in the leadership brought a departure from standard practice. Commander Grant had served out his time as skipper and accepted orders to be the air boss on USS *Lexington*. And I quickly learned VT-26's new commanding officer was cut from the same cloth as the Ops O across the street.

The new skipper enjoyed his position of power as well as the company of the entourage of junior officers who would have a drink with him at the Officers' Club after flying. I rarely went to the O Club for a drink, and if I did, I had a root beer. That was a strike against me. He also let it be known—and publicly—that he was no fan of girls in his Navy. Another strike. The irony was that he'd married a woman who had been enlisted in the Navy.

I had already completed the class, passed the test, and been placed on the flight schedule to get my gunnery qual when the new skipper's Ops O took my name off the list. Word spread—no guns for Bonnell. When I heard of the decision from my fellow instructors, who also repeated the Ops O's claim that "girls don't do guns in the skipper's Navy," I knew I'd been publicly labeled a second-class citizen. I went to the Ops O's office to have a private conversation.

"Why did you take my name off the list?" I asked. "And why am I hearing about this from my peers rather than from you?"

"It's because you snivel off too much."

The answer almost made me laugh. *Snivel off* was a Navy term for asking for time off. My only snivels were on Wednesday evenings to teach children's choir—a time of day when gunnery flights were never scheduled. The instructor who had been given my slot as a gunnery instructor had less time in the squadron than I did and sniveled off on a regular basis in the middle of the day to play basketball. I knew this because I was a scheduler. Besides, sniveling off was never a problem; we all had things other than flying to do, and we worked together to protect our outside interests.

When I pointed out these things about my colleague, the Ops O changed tactics. "He's going to use guns in the fleet, and you're not."

That argument didn't hold water either. There were a number of jets without guns in the fleet—the A-6, EA-6, and S-3—that he might end up flying. And while my opportunities were limited as a woman, I could still end up using gunnery tactics in an aggressor squadron. In that role I'd play the part of enemy aircraft to help train our fleet, and enemy aircraft had guns in their arsenal. The truth was, regardless of which jet any of us might be assigned, gunnery was dynamic flying and made all of us better pilots.

"Sir, to be clear, what you're saying is that I'm not going to get to fly guns because I'm a girl. You know that isn't fair."

"Give it up, Bonnell. It's decided. Skipper says he's not going to waste his advanced qual on a female. Write me up for discrimination if you want to."

I had no recourse. My complaint would go right up the chain of command to the person who had made the decision.

That was a devastating blow, and the fairness fairy inside of me was livid. But I reminded myself that life isn't always fair. It wasn't fair that my little sister had been born with cerebral palsy. It wasn't fair that when the economy turned bad in New Mexico, my father had to move halfway across the country without his family to find work. In the grand scheme of life, mine was a minor setback, and I wouldn't stoop to pouting. This was not going to derail my aviation career. Back then I didn't have a way to describe exactly what I felt. Today I would say I was no snowflake, and it would take much more than this to melt me.

I let things cool down for a week or so, then gave it one last shot. I went directly to the CO to plead my case, hoping to find him in a better frame of mind. Not only had he not changed his mind; he slapped me with a penalty. He assigned me an advanced qual no one wanted: Out of Control Flight (OCF).

As I've mentioned, OCF training is a necessary evil. No one likes it, but every student has to pass the flight before they can solo. Students learn how the aircraft feels as it approaches a stall so they can avoid it, and they learn how to recover if a departure from controlled flight occurs. Every OCF flight requires about ten departures. It begins with the tamer stalls, then progresses to the more animated departures, including rudder triplets and zero-airspeed entries that would send us spinning and flip-flopping around like the Zipper ride at the carnival. The combination of positive, negative, and even lateral g's all wreak havoc on a pilot's equilibrium. OCF students who are experiencing it for the first time often lose their lunch all over the cockpit. It's pretty dynamic and physically taxing enough that instructor pilots (IPs) were allowed to fly only one OCF per day. Considering all of this, it should come as no surprise that no IP ever *requested* to teach OCF.

This would be my lot for the next year, however, so I embraced it. Ultimately it was my responsibility to make sure we got through the flight safely, so I became intimately familiar with the Navy OCF manual and memorized every recovery listed. Our lives depended on it.

The aviation saying goes, "If you have altitude and airspeed, you still have a chance." Sometimes in OCF we had altitude but no airspeed, so I made up my own version: "If you have altitude and ideas, you still have a chance." With ideas, we could make our way out of trouble and back to flying safely.

It was rewarding to see students develop skills they had dreaded learning. Now, if their aircraft departed flight, they could recognize the symptoms and know the cure. It was also rewarding to help alleviate their dread of the training. The rumor mill had built up expectations about the OCF to the point where students were greenish and swallowing hard during the brief. Some instructors even made a point of trying to get their students to vomit, thinking that was a rite of passage. But watching someone else get sick had never made me feel better. And since I made it a point to help the plane captains clean up the cockpit whenever my students threw up, I was motivated to find a solution.

Fortunately I found one. Because everyone approached the flight with the foregone conclusion that they were going to throw up, they tended not to eat, thinking they'd throw up less. But we were required to fly with our oxygen masks on from takeoff to touchdown, and 100 percent oxygen under pressure on an empty stomach is a recipe for disaster.

I started looking up students the day before their OCF flight and encouraging them to eat *something*, ideally a peanut butter sandwich, before the brief. Then I'd dangle a carrot, promising them that after we finished the requirements of the flight, we would burn the rest of our gas doing something fun, like aerobatics or sightseeing.

It worked! That was pretty much the end of messy cockpits with my students. Being able to conquer OCF without "blowing chow" made them stand a little taller, and in the end it made my life easier.

Throughout that challenging year I stayed focused on the long game in life, remembering who I was and what I'd come to do. I think it's no coincidence that my future husband took note of me during this time, but not as a damsel in distress. When our paths finally crossed, I caught his attention as a confident woman with a can-do attitude who was having the time of her life.

CHAPTER 7

A FACE FOR
MR. WONDERFUL

I found him whom my soul loves.
—SONG OF SOLOMON 3:4

Though surrounded by a sea of men, many of whom were smart, athletic, and handsome, I rarely had a date. I simply hadn't met anyone I really liked who liked me back, and I certainly wasn't a "sport dater." Perhaps because I had healthy relationships with men during my formative years—with my dad, brothers, and their friends—I didn't feel the need to vie for men's attention. I had a few buddies on base, my housemates, and, above all, my family, who invested in me and I in them.

After earning my wings, I had rewarded myself with a German shepherd puppy and named him Huckleberry. Huck was a furry bundle of joy in my life. I started rushing home after work just to see him. My four-legged friend greeted me at the back screen door every day with a happy face and a wagging tail. He became my confidant and study partner who curled up beside me while I hit the books as a new instructor pilot.

Though I still hoped to share my life with a special two-legged someone, I wasn't in a hurry to find him. I did, of course, want that experience of loving someone and being loved back, of sharing a home of our own, of eventually becoming a mom. Normal stuff. My mental sketch of this man, which I had started as a younger woman, continued to develop but remained faceless. Like ideas of Mr. Wonderful, I also had an image in my head of the Perfect Mom I hoped to be—a mix of Mary Poppins and Maria von Trapp.

Since marriage and motherhood weren't areas of life that I could plan and plot, I would have to wait. But I just wasn't going to pine away while I waited. That wasn't in my DNA. There's always something worthwhile for a person to do to stay busy: I found out that in my church were children who needed a Sunday school teacher. Woodworking projects I enjoyed. Elderly friends who needed a hand with tasks I could do. Music and study and training and—my favorite—reading outside, sitting in the sun with a jug of ice-cold sweet tea. When my days as a flight-training student came to an end, I finally had more time for these things.

Every year, when I went home to New Mexico for Christmas, my family teased me a little bit about the lack of romance in my life. They never nagged, but questions like "Any boy we should know about?" and "What are you waiting for?" routinely found their way into the conversation. My answers were also routine:

"No, I haven't met anyone special."

"I *do* have fun, just not dating."

"I don't *need* anyone, but if I happen to meet Mr. Wonderful, you'll be the first to know. Until then, I've got Huck to keep me company."

When I went home for Christmas in 1987, however, there was no teasing—not even by my brothers. No one mentioned dating or romance or marriage at all. I was crestfallen. They'd given up! Suddenly I felt worried. Maybe I would never marry.

I headed back to Texas after Christmas was over, trying to focus on everything that was right with my life. Life was good—even for a spinster. But I wondered.

*   *   *

Not long after I first arrived in Beeville, I'd found a little church called New Life Baptist. About a hundred people attended each week. They welcomed me for being me, just Tammie Jo. I was included not for what I could give or do but because the people were genuinely friendly.

Pastor Santos Martinez introduced me to a few people. Right away the music director asked me to sing in the choir. He didn't seem to mind that the flight schedule would sometimes keep me from making Wednesday-night practices. When he found out I played the flute, he asked me to play during the offertories on Sunday mornings. My life soon took on a happy rhythm. I was becoming part of the church family, and I started making my home away from home.

The Sunday after I returned from that Christmas in New Mexico—January 3, 1988—I wore a new blue dress to church. As I sang in the choir, I noticed a young man come in the back and find a seat. I'd never seen him before. He was good-looking, and he seemed comfortable in church, relaxed and happy. That detail seemed to stick in my mind. Other aviators came to the church now and then, some because it was the only place in Beeville (besides a bar) to meet girls and some because they wanted to be part of the fellowship. This guy looked, well, genuine. He was plugged into the service, and, I admit, I thought him handsome. I worked with hundreds of handsome guys, but this didn't make me immune. It did, however, make me realize that good looks weren't everything.

After the service an intelligence officer from the base introduced us. This new young man's name was Dean Shults. He had just completed Primary Flight Training in Corpus Christi before the Christmas break and was assigned to Intermediate Jet Training in VT-26, where he would check in the next day. We exchanged hellos; then someone else who wanted to meet him interrupted us.

I didn't tell Dean I was an instructor in his squadron. I didn't even mention I was in the Navy.

That Monday our squadron had what's called a Safety Stand Down, where everyone takes a break from the routine of flying or fixing airplanes to refocus on safety. About 160 students and instructors were in the room, everyone in flight suits. I sat with the other instructors near the front, with a set of felt reindeer antlers on my head. Commander Fred Grant was still leading our squadron then. He and I had a friendly ongoing battle between his "bah, humbug" and my "happy elf" approach to Christmas. We didn't fool each other, though. He loved Christmas, and I loved his sense of humor, and we kept it up long after the holidays ended.

The meeting itself progressed on a serious note, and various department heads spoke. Commander Grant went last. A twinkle came to his eye as he stood in front of the ready room and said, "Well, all these guys have talked about it privately all day"—he pointed in my direction—"but none of them have been man enough to publicly mention Tammie Jo's *horniness*."

The room erupted in laughter. I ripped the antlers off my head and threw them at Commander Grant.

"They're antlers, not horns, sir!" I said.

That's how Ensign Shults learned I was an instructor in his squadron.

★   ★   ★

For a while after that, when Ensign Shults and I saw each other at church or passed in the ready room at the squadron, we would say hello, but we didn't spend any time together. He was busy with ground school and simulator training, and I was busy instructing.

When the time came for him to do his instrument cross-country, he and his three roommates planned to do them at the same time. The plan was to meet up at Holloman Air Force Base after the flights for a three-day weekend of snow skiing in Ruidoso, New Mexico, where Dean's dad had a cabin. His roommates had their instructors, but Dean's on-wing wasn't available, so he asked around and heard that I was from New Mexico and might be persuaded to go. He called me and explained the situation, told me who was going, and assured me that at the cabin I would have a bedroom and bath of my own. I liked to ski and loved the thought of going home to New Mexico, so I was happy to join the party.

The evening before the trip, I started receiving calls from the other instructors. One couldn't go because his student had gone med down. Another student hadn't finished all the prerequisite flights on time, so they were out. Then the phone rang again. The third instructor's girlfriend was coming to town, so he and his student had rescheduled. What started as a group of four planes and eight pilots had become a party of two. Ensign Shults and I were heading up to his father's cabin for a three-day weekend. Alone.

I was twenty-six years old and grown up enough to make my own decisions, yet I felt a little odd about how this was shaping up. I cared very much about protecting my "keep it clean" reputation—not just for me but for the girls coming through the program behind me.

I called my parents to ask for their advice. Normally they were pretty conservative, leaning toward prudish if truth be told, but to my surprise my mom and dad just laughed and said, "Oh, Tammie Jo. You'll always be the only girl on a trip. You're the only girl in your squadron. You like to ski. You like to fly. Go have fun."

Ensign Shults and I headed west on a cross-country to New Mexico. He seemed comfortable, a lot more at ease than I had been when I was a student. In fact, he was even more at ease than I was then as an instructor. I would eventually learn that Dean Shults has never met a stranger. He was and still is universally charming. But at the time I wondered if he felt like he had no choice but to be polite. After all, I was grading him.

We flew to El Paso first, then over to Holloman Air Force Base in Alamogordo, New Mexico, where we checked out a car from the motor pool. From there we drove the rest of the way up the mountain. The conversation flowed between us, but we kept it professional.

The cabin was cozy, an inviting home on stilts in a heavily wooded area. The weather was cold. Snow was falling. We headed indoors, stomped the snow off our flight boots, and I settled into my room while he settled into his. Both of us lived on tight budgets, so we didn't go out to eat that evening. We had stopped for groceries on the way up. Dinner was toasted cheese sandwiches with some fruit. And not by candlelight, not even close although, now that we were away from base, we started calling each other by our first names.

After dinner I went to my room to read. I was using a guide that directed my reading through the Bible in one year, so I picked up my Bible and started in where I'd left off the day before. It occurred to me that I was being a bit rude by cloistering myself in my room, so I went out to the living room, where I found Dean also reading. To my surprise he was also reading his Bible—and he was using the same reading guide. The discovery broke the ice and gave us something deeper than aviation to talk about.

Soon our conversation turned to what we'd done in high school and college, the depth of friendships we had found in some people, and what we valued most in a friend. I loved that he could talk about real life and not just sports or a TV show. (My TV knowledge was slim.) We talked about home, faith, and our journeys into aviation.

Dean and his two older brothers grew up near Houston, where he attended the largest high school in Texas. His father was an engineer, and his mother was a teacher until she became a stay-at-home mom. He was in junior high when his parents separated. Dean noticed how much better his brothers were handling this family trauma, so he asked them how they were doing it. Their answer: Jesus. The brothers hadn't grown up in church, but when their worlds were rocked, they reached for something, for Someone, that was solid and true. They introduced Dean to a campus Bible study, which is where he met Charles and Annie Towery, a couple who hosted Christian retreats on their farm outside of Houston and who became spiritual mentors to Dean.

Though we had our differences, the more we talked, the more we seemed to click, and it was more than our shared Christian faith, sense of humor, approach to people, or take on life. The click was *us*.

We went skiing the next day. Because we didn't have ski gear, we wore our flight suits with long johns underneath. Dean cracked jokes, we raced down the slopes, and we met up with some other pilots from the squadron who had driven up for the long weekend. It was a day of laughter. The next day was much the same, with a fresh layer of powder on the slopes.

I had already graded a few of Dean's flights, and he had done well although I'd been careful not to make my comments on his grade sheets too glowing. As a pilot, he was meticulous and attentive. It had been a pleasure to instruct him.

On the morning of our second day of skiing, Dean showed up with a handmade evaluation sheet for me. The topics were nonsensical and mostly had to do with my skiing.

"It's only fair," he told me.

I thought he had a lot of sass, but the grade sheet—and the handwritten creativity behind it—was an endearing work of art that I still keep in my jewelry box. As we skied our last run of the day, I thought about how good it felt to have a fun, lighthearted weekend with a fellow pilot. My heart tapped on my mind's door as if to bring news: *Dean is a very nice guy. His direction in life parallels yours.*

I wondered about that. I truly did. But most of the guys I knew in the Navy were looking for someone who could follow them. They were just getting started in a career that could send them in any one of a dozen directions after training, then somewhere else every two or three years. Trying to mesh two of those career paths in a relationship, let alone a marriage, just didn't seem practical.

I stepped back, put on my instructor hat, and we headed home to Texas.

* * *

Impracticality wasn't enough to keep Dean and me apart. After that cross-country trip we started finding excuses to do things together. We talked more at church, and our talks grew longer. We played racquetball and went to the same Bible study. When it seemed Dean might formally ask me on a date, I decided to speak to Commander Grant about it. Even though Dean wasn't my on-wing student, we were in the same squadron.

I went to the skipper's office and asked if he had time to chat. When he said yes, I stepped in and shut the door. He raised his eyebrows.

"It's about a guy," I said.

He pushed back from his desk. "Oh no."

"No. It's nothing bad."

"Well, lay it on me. What's going on?"

I sat down. "There's a student pilot I met at church. We flew a cross-country together and are starting to spend some time together. I think he may ask me out. I like him but don't want to do anything that would create a scandal of any kind."

Commander Grant stood, came around from behind his desk, and sat beside me.

"Tammie Jo," he said, "in order for there to be a scandal,

someone of importance has to be involved." He remained quiet long enough for the humor of his statement to sink in. "I'm the commanding officer, and I'm married. If I dated a student, that would be a scandal. Neither one of you is important enough to create a scandal. I suggest you not kiss him in the ready room. Tell whoever you want—or don't tell anyone at all because your peers will give you grief. If you fly with him, I know you're professional enough to grade him fairly."

So that was that.

It was February 1988. Dean and I had known each other for less than two months. And for our first official date, Dean took me to a George Winston piano concert in another town. Because music is my one weakness, Dean's choice set him apart. It signaled to me that he was willing to put some money and effort into a date—specifically, *our* date. He wore a sport coat, and I wore my nicest dress. I loved that he felt at ease in more than a flight suit.

We took care not to be public about our relationship and went about our business professionally. We rarely even spoke, much less held hands, in the squadron or even on base. At church and at Bible study, we quietly took seats next to each other and acted like any other newly dating couple. The first time Dean casually put his arm around me at New Life Baptist, the song leader actually lost his place mid-song! Our covert operation in church was over.

I told my parents about Dean, and they wavered between skeptical and relieved. I met his next oldest brother and his wife, Gary and Susan. They were as warm and wonderful as he had described them.

Dean had his practical side, but he could be romantic too. Sometimes the two mixed. Once, he asked to borrow my car for a trip to San Antonio. It was still winter, and my car's tires were nearly bald. When he came back from his trip, my car had four new tires. To me, that selfless and expensive gift showed he was thinking of my safety, but it felt like more than that. He was investing in me with more than his time and smiles.

On Friday nights Dean came to my house out in the country. We popped popcorn and watched classic movies. I loved Audrey Hepburn, Jimmy Stewart, Doris Day, Charlton Heston, and Fred Astaire. Several happy weeks went by like this until one Friday evening when Dean didn't show. He didn't even call. I was indignant.

The next morning he called and asked, "Can I come by and see you?"

I said I was too busy. He wouldn't give up. He could tell my feelings were hurt, and he knew why.

"I can't tell you yet why I wasn't there, but I promise it was for a good reason."

I relented. He came over, and he talked. I listened. But he remained strangely elusive about why he had missed our movie night.

*   *   *

Within months Dean wanted to meet my folks. The request stirred up questions, but I kept them inside. We went to New Mexico, and the weekend seemed to go well, though Dean didn't say much on the way home. I wondered how he truly felt about me and my family.

Dean had gone to Texas A&M University, and it seemed like he knew someone in every Texas town. Every weekend he had a new set of family friends he wanted me to meet. The most precious to him were Charles and Annie—the older couple who had spent a lot of time investing in, loving, and mentoring him as a young adult.

When we arrived at their home, I was given my own cozy room and bath. The next morning Dean came bursting into my room with a cup of coffee for me. He plopped down beside me on top of the bed and ruffled my hair all over my head. I thought, *This is nice. This is the way I'd like to wake up every morning.* Those thoughts were so unlike me! But the more I thought about it, the more I knew a change had come over me.

That image of Mr. Wonderful that I had sketched and carried around with me in my head since childhood suddenly had a face, and it was Dean's. He was a gentleman. He measured up to the real men in my life—my dad, my brothers, and some of my peers. I hadn't met many I considered to be of their caliber and, until that moment, hadn't fallen in love with any of them.

While we were visiting Annie and Charles, Dean came down with a head cold. That weekend he lay on the couch in their family room, recuperating, and I sat on the floor and chatted with him for hours. He rolled over and kissed me on the cheek.

This was our first kiss. Not a Hollywood kiss, but an I-like-you kiss. I have thought about that kiss often. As brief as it was, it changed my world forever. Dean wasn't a passing fancy, and he wasn't simply a friend. He loved me. He thought I was funny and cute. He thought all the things a girl wants her beau to think, and I felt the same about him.

It was so nice to have him champion me and to be the one to champion him. If one of us got sick, we'd be there for each other. There was a couch and a blanket waiting—and, for better or worse, one of us would always be the keeper of the other on that couch. I liked that. I truly did.

One day in July, after Dean had finished T-2s and moved on

to A-4s, he said, "Hey, this weekend I want you to meet my uncle Ted and aunt Velma." They lived on the Sabinal River in Utopia, Texas, a couple of hours away.

I wasn't sure I could go to Utopia. My little brother, D'Shane, was staying with me that summer. He was fifteen, and we were catching up. Due to our age difference, I'd missed most of his childhood. I also had duty at the squadron. But Dean was insistent, even adamant, that we *had* to go that weekend. So I traded shifts with a friend, and Dean, D'Shane, and I headed to Utopia.

After dinner Dean asked me if I'd like to go for a boat ride down the river. D'Shane piped up and said that sounded like fun, but a glance went between Uncle Ted and Dean, and Uncle Ted said, "Why don't you and I go tomorrow morning, D'Shane? I'll show you some good fishing holes."

It was growing dark when Dean and I headed out in the little boat. We paddled down a beautiful part of the river with big cypress trees hanging over the water. A full moon was out and brilliant in the clear night sky. Dean said he had written something for me. He pulled out a piece of paper and began to read a poem. It was beautiful, funny, and poignant, lines meant only for me. Before he finished, he knelt down in the boat and said the last line from memory: "Tammie Jo, will you marry me?" In Dean's outstretched hand was a diamond ring. All I needed to do was say yes.

"Did you ask my dad?" The question came out before I thought about the words.

"Yes," Dean said. "That weekend we went to New Mexico to visit them." *So that's why Dean was so quiet on the way home.* "Remember that weekend I missed our movie night? I was buying your ring. I didn't want to give it to you until I was finished in the squadron."

"You knew you wanted to marry me all the way back in March?"

Dean grinned. "When you know . . . you just know."

He had kept the ring hidden for four months. Four months! I looked at the moon. Dean had known all along that night was going to be a full moon. He remembered that I'd told him how much I loved moonlight—how when I was young I used to sit outside on top of the haystack or on a favorite post by our salt cedar pond and watch the moon rise over the Sacramento Mountains.

"If you don't say yes, I'm going to turn the boat over," he teased.

I murmured my assent, and when I kissed Dean then, it was no small kiss on the cheek. That's all you need to know.

★   ★   ★

We set our wedding date for Thanksgiving weekend in 1988, eleven months after we first met. Career-wise, we were reaching the time when we would both be getting new orders, and to military detailers, engagement is of no consequence. If you're married, however, they'll try to keep you as close as possible to each other when they consider assignments. We did *not* want to be detailed to opposite coasts.

It was a busy four months. Our church and friends helped with preparations. My mom made the butter mints, pralines, and satin flowers that held birdseed for guests to toss with their farewells. Dean's mom bought the only floral arrangement other than my bouquet. My parents paid for my dress, which I designed and had sewn by a lovely seamstress in Brownsville.

Just a few weeks before the wedding, I took a student up for his out-of-control flight. My idea of fun had changed a bit with time and so many departures under my belt. I'd even started to laugh at the other OCF instructors' jokes about falling out of the sky—jokes that no one else thought were funny.

My student was squared away. In the brief it was clear he knew his stuff, and it was a beautiful day. As we walked out to the jet, I was thinking this might be a day we could "light a fire"—my term for a particularly fun way to depart a controlled flight. It could be done only on nice calm-wind days. I explained the maneuver to him. After flying straight up with a perfectly steady 90 degrees, nose high, the aircraft would reach zero airspeed and we'd begin to slide backward. If we could maintain the aircraft at 90 degrees, the engines would ignite the residual fuel in the trail of exhaust as we slid backward through it. The flame would surround the cockpit for a flash of a moment. It took 30 percent talent and 70 percent luck to light a fire, but it was an engaging challenge that was just for fun, not for a grade.

As our jet climbed toward twenty-nine thousand feet, I asked the student a few questions, and he was well prepared with answers. I started the OCF with a few basic stalls to burn the fuel out of the tip tanks on the ends of the wings and to get him accustomed to the eerie feeling of a stall entry. These first maneuvers were always pretty docile. By the time the stalls were finished, the tip tank fuel was burned off and we could start the more dynamic departures and spins.

During the brief, we had agreed that if he hadn't recovered the aircraft by eighteen thousand feet, I would take over the controls. This was routine. Whoever wasn't flying would call out the altitude as we descended to keep us both cognizant of where we were in the sky and how fast the ground was rising. I was usually the one calling out altitudes until the student recovered: "Twenty-five . . . twenty-four . . . twenty-three . . . twenty-two—excellent!

Nice job! I have the controls," and we would head back up to twenty-eight thousand feet, where I would fly us into the next departure and hand the controls over to the student for recovery.

Our first maneuver was a clean stall, done with the gear and flaps up. It was the tamest of the maneuvers and was started by pulling the power to idle and simply holding altitude as the airspeed bled off. The rudder pedals would shudder, and the stall warning horn would sound. At the point the aircraft stalled, the nose would drop, and students would recover the aircraft by relaxing pressure on the stick and positively neutralizing the controls as they added power. My student followed the proper procedures, but instead of a lull in aircraft control and an easy drop of the nose, the plane whipped down and around, and the nose headed straight at the ground.

We were at about twenty-eight thousand feet when the plane entered a spiral, catching us completely off guard. A spiral is abnormal for the T-2 and quite violent. We'd practiced spins, *not* spirals. A spin maintains a pretty steady 90 knots as the aircraft circles downward in a flat "falling leaf" type of descent. The scenery from the cockpit is going sideways, and it's a dynamic but not a violent maneuver. But in this spiral we were headed straight down in a twisting motion, increasing speed with every turn. The aircraft was shuddering so hard it was difficult to focus our eyes on the instruments. I took control of the aircraft immediately, and he called out the altitude: "Twenty-five."

The spiral tightened up. We were aiming for the ground like a drill bit. This little straight-winged Buckeye wasn't supposed to be able to go into a spiral. We didn't even have procedures to get out of one! I tried every combination of recovery inputs, but nothing worked.

"Twenty. Nineteen. Eighteen. Seventeen . . ." The plane was

unresponsive to me and gaining speed. The instruments became a blur, but I could make out the airspeed and redline needles as they grew closer and closer together. The plane vibrated and rattled. The noise grew intense. The student kept calling out altitudes as we passed them. "Fourteen. Thirteen. Twelve! *Eleven!*" The lower the numbers became, the higher in pitch his voice grew. We hurtled toward the ground at about four hundred miles per hour.

I tried everything I could think of. Since there were no recovery procedures for this situation in our manuals, I felt like a test pilot at this point. We passed ten thousand feet. If we weren't in control by the time we hit five thousand, we would have to eject.

The ejection procedures flashed through my mind. There were two handles I could pull—a handle between my legs (the quickest method) or another handle over my head, which was more prudent to grab if I had time. This handle was attached to a fabric shield that protects the pilot's face and draws the arms against the body. Little things mean a lot when a rocket is kicking you in the rear out of an aircraft traveling four hundred miles per hour! (The back seat would fire a split second ahead of the front so we wouldn't hit each other in the air.)

We were a couple of seconds from ejecting. My student belted out the altitude a little more shrilly than before: *"Eight! Seven! Six!"*

The adrenaline rush took over. My mind was racing as fast as the spiraling plane, but none of the thoughts seemed hurried or rushed at all.

Really, God? I'm getting married soon, and ejections are messy! I'll be a bruised and lacerated bride who would frighten Frankenstein! The announcements are out. We can't change the date. I'll be a monster in a big white dress . . . and they only take wedding pictures once. On the wedding day!

I was so annoyed I kicked the rudders—stomped on them. Left! Right! Left! I threw the stick forward and reached for the ejection handle.

The plane wobbled out of the spiral.

"Don't. Touch. Anything." I said in my most calm and authoritative voice. The student had the same ejection handles that I did, and I wanted to land in the plane, not in a parachute.

The plane bottomed out, well below five thousand feet. We were flying in control again. All was smooth for a moment, and neither of us said a word. Then I thought, *If we don't complete this flight, he's going to have a hard time getting back in the aircraft to do it again.* So I briefed him as we climbed back up. I told him he might have had some flight-control inputs that he wasn't aware of that prompted us to spiral.

"Let's try it again," I instructed. "Just be really gentle with the nose and keep your ailerons neutral."

He didn't say anything—I couldn't blame him—but he didn't object as we climbed.

We flew up to twenty-nine thousand feet again and repeated the exercise. This time the plane did as it should: a lovely, wonderful, just-what-you'd-expect stall. The student recovered in textbook style, and we continued with the flight, going through the rest of the departures into stalls or spins without any surprises.

When we landed, he bent down and kissed the ground. Right then and there, in front of God and everyone.

I found the skipper and told him about our flight. He had never heard of a T-2 going into a spiral. We looked for any information on T-2s and spirals but couldn't find any. The student and I stood our ground when others started questioning our description of the flight.

I called the Navy's test-pilot school at NAS Patuxent River

and described the flight. A pilot who had flown extensive tests in the T-2 agreed the plane had spiraled. He said, "Well, it is rare because the only way to make a T-2 spiral is to stall it with a significant asymmetrical load."

With some investigation and help from maintenance, we learned that one of the tip-tank valves in our T-2 was sticking, causing that tank to drain extremely slowly. When we did our first stall, there had been about five hundred more pounds of fuel at that end of the wing. That's what had caused our asymmetrical moment.

Pax River faxed me the recovery procedures for a spiral, and I committed them to memory. Maintenance also assured me that they were checking those valves in every aircraft. That was comforting, but from then on I avoided that particular airplane—just out of principle.

Years later I saw that same student on the flight line at NAS Miramar. If I remember correctly, my squadron was working with TOPGUN, and he was going through some training. He gave me a big bear hug right in front of his buddies. He didn't even introduce me before he launched into a hilarious retelling of our adventure. He didn't miss a detail and had us all in stitches, even reenacting the part where he kissed the ground after landing.

What he didn't know was that I had also kissed the ground . . . out of sight—so as not to scare my next student.

★ ★ ★

Dean and I hosted our rehearsal dinner at a small Mexican restaurant in town. We had arranged for a simple dinner party of thirty, but I think the owner and his family took pity on us—a couple of kids who obviously were pressed for time and low on funds and creativity. They pulled out all the stops, surprising us with piñatas and a mariachi band. The owner's daughters danced for us in beautiful, flowing Mexican dresses. Afterward the entire wedding party went to the church to help finish decorating. My college roommate Kandy Johnson gave bow-tying lessons to Janice Blakeman, Arlene Fender, and me as we all pitched in to finish the church trimming. It was late when we declared the church ready.

At the end of this long day, Dean drove me back to my place. He had planned the honeymoon but still hadn't told me exactly where we were staying or what kind of clothes to pack—for warm climate or snow. He parked the car, took my hand, and said, "I just want you to know I have no reservations—"

I came unglued. I did not merely melt down; I was angry. I had coordinated all the details of the wedding with no family nearby, no wedding planner, no florist—just me. I was near exhaustion. Like most brides, I had wanted the event to be a reflection of what was important to me.

"You have *no reservations*? I'm planning the wedding and instructing and scheduling full-time while moving into a new home, and you do not have reservations for the honeymoon?"

He gave me a quizzical look. He'd never seen me this upset. "About marrying you," he said. "I have no reservations about marrying you."

I sat quietly for a while. He was quiet too, and he simply took my hand and held it. Slowly a faint smile came to my face. I loved him so much. Particularly now, in this horrible moment. He hadn't left me. He hadn't yelled back. *So this is real love*, I thought. *This is my Dean and how he handles life.*

Although he had no reservations about marrying me, Dean did have reservations in Hawaii. We spent a week on Maui, and our honeymoon was fabulous, just as honeymoons should be. We dined at a luau on the beach. We went body surfing in the warm ocean waters. We drove through Hawaii's majestic rain forests, and we meandered across sandy beaches.

Early one morning while it was still dark, we drove to the top of a mountain in Maui and watched the sunrise. I'd seen hundreds of sunrises. Even as a teenager, I would get up early to watch them, but this one stands out because it was my first sunrise with Dean. *My* Dean.

CHAPTER 8

OPEN HOSTILITY

*We never accepted that it was okay for "girls"
to accept a lower standard, to expect less of
themselves than men. Like so many of life's
achievements, the key [to progress] is simple
perseverance.*

—COMMANDER ROSEMARY MARINER, *LOS ANGELES TIMES*

Dean not only understood my world; he understood me. That was a powerful combination that I could lean on when I faced opposition meant to stop my progress.

We spent our first Christmas together in Beeville and hosted the church singles party in our ancient little rental house. Life at my squadron resumed a pleasant rhythm of teaching classes and doing some fun flying. Dean went to the Happy Batt, VT-24, and was enjoying every minute in the A-4. After work, if Dean brought a friend over to study, I would have cinnamon toast and hot cocoa ready.

When I finished my SERGRAD tour and Dean earned his wings of gold, we moved to California—but not to the same city. He received orders to VA-122, the A-7 Replacement Air Group (RAG) in Lemoore, and I was assigned 250 miles south to VAQ-34 in Point Mugu, one of only two "electronic aggressor" squadrons in the Navy. They were also the only two squadrons where women could fly tactical aircraft on tactical missions—just not in combat.

For the next couple of years, Dean and I were seldom with each other for more than a few days at a time. A week at the most. I was gone on detachments to Hawaii, Puerto Rico, and NAS Miramar for several weeks in a row. He was out at sea for six months. We had no cell phones or e-mail—nothing except landlines and snail mail. Usually it was me flying one place and him flying some other place, with us talking on the phone in the meantime, always seeking to connect.

In spite of the distance from Dean, I was happy about my assignment to VAQ-34 for a number of reasons, one of which was that my squadron's executive officer was Commander Rosemary Mariner. She had been in the first class of women in the Navy to earn wings of gold in 1974. Ever since then she had shown herself to be a champion of *people*, not just women. Her brilliance and incredible work ethic were the signature qualities of her time as our leader. One of the things I admired most about her was that she was never reactionary but always thoughtful and measured in her response.

The squadron also had other ladies of different ranks and occupations. When I taught, I had met two women coming through as students, Gretchin Daobe and Kara Hultgreen. Other than that, I had never been attached to a squadron with other women, so it was nice not to be the odd woman out. With Commander Mariner as number two in the squadron, she and the commanding officer set a great tone. It felt more like a graduate-level group working on a mission. There were no fiefdoms.

After having spent about a month getting settled into VAQ-34 and loving it, it was time to hit the road to start my list of classes and training for the VAQ mission. The first stop was at Electronic Warfare School, and the first thing that caught my attention was that it was in a windowless building behind a razor-wire-topped fence. Getting into the building was only the first challenge. For three weeks I packed my brain with data about the electronic warfare technology and capabilities of Russian, French, and Chinese weapons systems, because those were the suppliers to most of the bad guys around the world. Nothing like starting my new job with some mental gymnastics.

From there I headed for a camping trip with purpose: SERE (Survival, Evasion, Resistance, and Escape) School. The Navy was not equipped to handle women in its SERE School, so I went to Spokane, Washington, to train with the Air Force. After sitting in a windowless building for three weeks, SERE School was literally a breath of fresh air. We spent several days in the classroom, then headed out to put into practice what we had been learning.

The first few days in the field were all about how to survive and evade in hopes of not becoming a POW. The last few days were about how to *be* a POW. We learned techniques for resisting the enemy and also possible ways to escape. I was the senior ranking officer, so I was the leader of my half of the class, my forty survivors-turned-POWs.

The experience opened my eyes.

Until SERE School I had remained pretty neutral about women being in combat squadrons. I had just gotten married and spent a lot of my thoughts and energies on ways to stay on the same coast as Dean. Now SERE School demanded all of my attention. I was challenged and got an education in how men and women—including myself—respond to extremely stressful conditions under intense pressure.

Some argue that women shouldn't be allowed to serve in the military at all, or in certain positions, because they're not physically as strong as men or because in a POW situation they're more likely to be sexually assaulted. My time in SERE School taught me that neither of those arguments is completely valid. I saw a strong male college graduate—an officer who fit the classic profile of "America's finest"—almost wash out of the program because he couldn't handle the pressure of a POW training exercise. During that same exercise, a female enlistee with only her high school diploma took everything the instructors dished out at her. She'd come straight from inner-city Chicago, and she proved to be one of the toughest people physically as well as mentally—male or female—that I had ever met. As for women being vulnerable to sexual assaults as POWs, we learned that sexual assault and humiliation are not tactics reserved only for women.

To be clear, I also saw firsthand in the SERE program that not everybody is cut out for combat. There are men who are and men who aren't. Likewise, there are women who are and women who aren't. Being prepared to engage the enemy in combat takes a certain mentality that is not gender specific.

SERE School helped me settle many of the questions I had been asking myself about women serving in the military. I left Spokane encouraged and inspired. From that point on I didn't have any doubt that women could handle combat in aviation.

★   ★   ★

As part of VAQ-34, I was sent to Naval Air Station Lemoore, where Dean was already stationed, to start training in the A-7 Corsair. That was something I had been looking forward to for months. My excitement, however, was short-lived. When I arrived at the squadron, I immediately felt like I was walking into an enemy camp. It was the most hostile environment I had ever experienced, and it started at the top.

Shortly after I arrived, the magazine *Aviation Week* came out with a story about female A-7 pilots. There were only a handful of us at the time, and the cover featured a photo of two of them in front of the aircraft. Before a ready room full of instructors and students, including me—the only woman in the squadron and present in the room—the XO ripped off the cover, crumpled it up, pretended to wipe his rear with it, and threw it on the ground.

"That's what I think of women flying A-7s," he said.

From then on instructors and students alike shied away or avoided eye contact with me. Those who went further and chose to be ugly toward me were safe in assuming their behavior would be supported.

One instructor pilot, whom I will refer to simply as Black Socks, went with me and several other students and instructors on a detachment from Lemoore down to NAF El Centro, where my bombs had been painted pink a couple of years earlier. We spent several days there doing fam (familiarization) and form (formation) flights.

During the brief for the flight back to Lemoore, I noticed Black Socks would never look me in the eyes. When a person won't look you in the eyes, something is up: maybe deception, maybe hatred, maybe worse. Up to that point my intuition about that had always proven to be true.

Guys like the XO and Black Socks seemed to hang their egos on the fact that they were naval aviators, and they couldn't stomach the thought of a woman flying their "man's" jet. I think it put a chink in their macho armor. I simply did not view life that way. I never associated my "girl card" with my pilot's license, regardless of what aircraft I flew.

The flight home was going to be a two-plane formation flight, and despite the chilly atmosphere in the brief, I was eager to get up in the air. I still loved formation. I had taught it for two years; it was like comfort food for me.

When I got to the maintenance counter, I was surprised to see Black Socks switching our jets. I was new to the fleet's way of doing things, but I hadn't seen this done by other instructors. The aircraft that maintenance assigned to you was the one you took. But he was the instructor, and I was the student. What was I going to say? "Hey, gimme back my jet!"? I had only about seven hours of flight time in the A-7 anyway, so I didn't have a favorite. *Whatever*, I thought. He could have his pick.

According to the syllabus, I was the lead aircraft on that flight, and Black Socks was my wingman. We launched out of El Centro, did our work in the clear blue skies over Southern California, then headed to Lemoore, where there was a storm brewing. By the time we arrived, the weather was below landing minimums, so we entered a holding pattern to wait it out. We stayed at high altitude to save fuel, but the winds up there were blowing at well over a hundred miles an hour, directly across our holding pattern. That required me to crab, or turn into the wind, and make constant adjustments to stay in the holding airspace.

All was going well until my plane's primary flight instruments died. That left me with a condition called "partial panel." For my aircraft altitude display, I had only a "peanut gyro," a small backup altitude indicator down by my right knee. For my heading, I had only a magnetic compass, which was bouncing around so erratically with the rough ride that I could only estimate my general direction.

This was a serious emergency, particularly considering my limited time in the jet and the fact that we were soon going to be in some thick goo—Navy slang for flying in dense clouds. I let Black Socks know about my situation and passed him the lead. Had I been alone, or had the roles been reversed and I was with an inexperienced student in that situation, I would have headed to an airport with clear skies. But Black Socks made a different choice.

He took the lead and let me know that we would stay put, and when the weather got above the minimums, we would land at Lemoore as planned. While not my first choice, I was okay with it because all I had to do was simply fly in tight formation. We continued to hold.

While the winds were still raging, Black Socks got a call from Center (air traffic control) that he was out of the holding airspace and needed to get back into it or risk conflicting with other aircraft in the area. He made the necessary adjustment. This happened a second time, and again Center directed him to return to the designated holding airspace. Considering the strong winds he was fighting, I didn't fault him. He had his hands full, and I was just hanging on to his wing, knowing I would need to hang on even tighter when we descended into the storm.

Finally the weather improved just enough. The field had opened up, but there was still about twenty-eight thousand feet of horrible weather between us and the ground. As soon as we left holding, we were going to be in the clouds, and we wouldn't break out until we were just two hundred feet above the ground, where we would be met with howling winds and a driving rainstorm.

In a partial panel situation it was procedure for the flight lead to fly the approach until the runway was in sight, then drop the wingman off "on the ball," or the visual glide slope. The flight lead's primary responsibility was to get his wingman to a place where he could take over visually and land. Unfortunately that was not what Black Socks had in mind—not even close.

Center gave us a descent and vectors toward the field, then handed us off to Approach. As soon as Black Socks checked in with Approach, they asked him if we would be doing a section approach (together) or separating for single approaches to the parallel runways. Without hesitation he said single and jinked away. Not seeing that coming and already in the goo, I immediately lost sight of him.

They hadn't even given Black Socks a new heading, and he had said nothing to me about individual approaches. I was shocked and disoriented. Switching from flying formation to flying instruments when you know it's coming is disorienting enough. When you don't know it is coming and you don't have any instruments but a peanut gyro—that's a recipe for vertigo. I couldn't wrap my mind around the fact that my instructor had just abandoned me to fend for myself in the thick of a storm in an emergency situation.

Black Socks hadn't bothered to get me lined up with the runway on a final approach course, so Lemoore Approach was going to have to talk me down. I immediately told them I was partial panel and would need a "no gyro" approach, meaning rather than giving me headings to fly, they would have to give me a direction, left or right, and tell me to "start turn . . . stop turn" to get me pointed in the right direction. Rocking around in the thick of a storm and blind to which way was up or down was a true test of my mettle.

The controller didn't miss a beat. She was a consummate professional and immediately began to talk me closer toward the runway, one point at a time. Increase descent, decrease descent. Start turn, stop turn. Step-by-step she lined me up with the runway and led me onto the glide path. When I put my landing gear and flaps down, I also lowered the hook. The runways in Lemoore all had arresting cables for emergencies such as mine. A-7s didn't handle well on wet runways, so it was standard procedure to "trap" if the runway had standing water. It was pouring rain. The runway would be covered in standing water.

As I headed down final approach, my whole world was a peanut gyro and the voice of the controller. I didn't waste a moment of thought on Black Socks. Just before I hit the altitude at which I would have had to decide to push the throttle up and make another pass, I started to make out a runway through the rain-swept windscreen. This was at least more familiar territory. I had the meatball on the left side of the runway for my glide slope, a runway for lineup, and my angle-of-attack indicator was working for airspeed. I thought I was home free.

I flew the meatball all the way to touchdown, hitting the runway as if I were on the deck of an aircraft carrier. My hook was down, and as I crossed the arresting cable, I felt my jet decelerate, but I didn't come to stop. Instead the jet jerked sideways, and I found myself sliding toward the right side of the runway. At that point, my brakes were useless, and returning to the air was not an option. I was along for the ride, and the ride left me sunk in the mud off the side of the runway.

★   ★   ★

Later, when I was getting checked out at the base medical clinic, as protocol dictated, the CO of VA-122 and his boss, the admiral in charge of all the A-7 and F/A-18 squadrons on the West Coast, stopped by. When I told them the story, the admiral smiled and said, "This isn't the first time an A-7 has ended up in the mud. The only difference between your story and mine was that when I slid off the runway, I kept sliding all the way across the grass and ended up on a taxiway. I taxied back to the ramp, parked the jet, and acted like nothing happened."

The CO, on the other hand, wasn't smiling or telling stories. He was silent and seemed less than amused.

Everything checked out fine at medical, and I was back in the squadron the next day. Over the next two days, meetings were held. Questions were asked. "How did this happen? *Why* did this happen?" The investigation was standard for every incident of this type.

I was careful not to denigrate Black Socks, and I tried to give him the benefit of the doubt. Circumstances in the air had been bad, and I couldn't blame him for that. Something must have happened that required him to abandon me. But Black Socks had a different approach; he insisted that I couldn't handle my aircraft even before I landed.

At one point he said, "Well, I knew she was a weak student when she was blown out of the holding pattern."

I did a double take. *He* had been in the lead. He was the one who had been blown out of the holding pattern!

He ended his testimony with, "She called me when she ran off the runway."

I longed to speak, but the CO was in charge of the hearing and never asked my side of the story.

Dean was away on a detachment the entire time. I called and told him my story, and he encouraged me. As a student, however, he had no more authority in the squadron than I did. There was nothing he could do.

After the inquiry on the second day, the maintenance officer—a lieutenant commander of equal rank to an Ops O—called me down to his office. He had been present at the hearing and said, "There were a number of times during the hearing that the look on your face made me think you had something to say. I'd like to hear it."

"Sir, with all due respect, I really don't know why Black Socks would throw me under the bus. I'm the one who ran off the runway," I said. I told him I was partial panel and had given Black Socks the lead. He was the one who was getting blown out of the holding pattern.

"You were partial panel?" the maintenance officer asked. He told me he hadn't heard anything about that, not even in the hearing. He advised me to go straight to maintenance control and make an entry in the aircraft logbook. Then he said, "If I were you, I would contact ATC and get a copy of the tape; then I would confront Black Socks. He knows what he did was wrong. That's why he's deflecting the attention to you."

This was the first conversation I'd ever had with the maintenance officer. We weren't friends, but when I left that meeting, I felt like I at least had an advocate.

I never sat in on another meeting about the incident, and within days I was back in the cockpit. I got wind that Black Socks was spreading poison about me around the squadron, and this revelation crushed me. But, as usual, my mom and dad had sage advice. They simply said, "Consider the source and move on." I took that on board, buried my head in the books, and kept flying.

My Bible reading tended toward a Psalm 35 flavor of encouragement, and as in the past, I realized I needed to pour out my heart and hurt and leave it before the Lord. I needed to keep my head clear and my heart healthy as well. As many people have said in various ways, resentment can be like drinking poison and waiting for the other person to get sick. Jesus warned against unforgiveness—for my own good, not His (Matthew 6:15; 18:35).

I did what the maintenance officer recommended and ordered a copy of the ATC tapes from the flight with Black Socks. When I finished the A-7 syllabus and was ready to head back to Point Mugu, I asked Black Socks if I could speak to him privately. We were in the ready room with others, and even though I tried to be discreet, you could have heard the proverbial pin drop. He and I went into a briefing room, and I played the tape of his conversations with Center during our flight.

I asked him, "Why did you say I was blown out of the holding pattern when it was you?"

He said nothing and walked out of the briefing room.

★ ★ ★

Years later I would learn that my XO at VAQ-34, Commander Mariner, had become aware of the Black Socks incident, seen that there was foul play afoot within the squadron, and acted behind the scenes to make sure an outside investigation was conducted.

They had concluded there was "no pilot error" in the incident, but all I'd known at the time was that I'd been cleared to continue flying in the program. I eventually received my 1,000-hour mishap-free award. I was proud of that then, but there would come a day when it would become even more significant to me.

That wasn't the only time Commander Mariner intervened on my behalf. While we were still in A-7 training at VA-122, Dean and I learned that the commanding officer, the same CO who hadn't had any questions for me at the hearing, was making arrangements for Dean to be assigned to an A-7 squadron on the East Coast. That didn't make any sense because Dean was one of few, if any, A-7 students who actually wanted to stay in Lemoore. The A-7s on the East Coast were based in Jacksonville, Florida, which was far more attractive to young and mostly single Navy pilots. The CO did not explain why he wanted to separate us, and we could only assume his motivation was less than honorable.

Since staying on the same coast was so important to us, I called Commander Mariner and asked if I could transfer to a squadron on the East Coast. She, of course, asked why, and after I explained, she told me she needed to look into the details. She never told me how she did it, but somehow she was able to keep Dean in Lemoore. That was truly remarkable since Dean was not in her command and she was junior to the CO of VA-122. She won a battle with a senior officer and could have easily boasted about it, but she didn't. Again, she had quietly taken care of her people without any fanfare.

Although it worked out in the end, my experiences with VA-122 shook me up. Why did my presence elicit such open hostility? What had I done to invite it? I realized that my welcome, or lack of welcome, in a squadron was completely dependent on the leadership, which was sure to change every couple of years. I had to remind myself that my value was based solely on what God, not man, thought of me. Standing on that truth, I could weather the storms that seemed to continually roll in over the horizon.

★   ★   ★

As a VAQ pilot, I had flown an abbreviated A-7 syllabus, with minimal training in the phases I did fly and no training at all in weapons, ACM, or carrier landings—in other words, none of the fun stuff. So even though I arrived in VA-122 a few months later than Dean, the timing happened to work out for us to finish A-7 training on the same day. The very next day, Dean was on a flight to Hawaii to join his new squadron for a six-month cruise.

Welcome to life in the fleet.

Though Dean and I were flying the same type of aircraft, our jobs were different. He was assigned to a carrier-based light-attack squadron where the mission was to put bombs on target in enemy territory. My squadron was shore based, and our role was to help promote the combat readiness of the fleet. We simulated enemy aircraft and missiles and attacked our own ships as well as other aircraft to help train combat pilots (men at the time) and the ships' weapons-systems operators. We were electronic aggressors, which meant we carried jamming pods and simulated enemy radar. In other words, we played the bad guys.

In those days, the late 1980s and early 1990s, the combat exclusion policy was still in place. This meant women were excluded from serving in units that went into combat. However, the Navy was ahead of the other US Armed Forces in allowing women to fly combat aircraft. In that regard I was fortunate that the Air Force and Army had turned me down.

I wasn't looking to break any barriers, and I didn't chafe at my assignment to an aggressor squadron. In fact, I thought I had won the lottery. It was the only place I could go and fly something as cool as an A-7. I also understood the importance of the aggressor squadrons' role. Somebody had to help train the fleet, and I was happy to be part of that team.

It seemed to me that the military would want to have the best fighting force no matter the race or gender of its members. Even thirty years ago we could feel the culture shift beginning throughout the military. Eventually the combat exclusion policy would be lifted from aviation positions, initially by Secretary of Defense Les Aspin on April 28, 1993. The Navy—just like all branches of the US military—had some turbulence leading up to and implementing this change. Aviation was the first door to open.

But when polarizing opinions are involved, not everybody changes or grows at the same speed.

★ ★ ★

Commander Mariner soon advanced from XO to CO of VAQ-34. Her promotion to skipper was a monumental event because she was the first woman ever to command an aviation squadron in our nation's history. In light of the historic moment, the change-of-command ceremony featured more than the usual pomp and circumstance.

When Commander Mariner learned that I was a singer, she asked me to perform "The Star Spangled Banner" at the ceremony. Senators, astronauts, and more admirals than I could count came to the event, and so did my parents and sister, Sandra. When Mom and Sandra arrived on base, they looked west with wide eyes. It was the first time they had ever seen an ocean. Mom's first comment was "It's so loud." They watched in amazement as a sea lion trolled along near the shore, then a school of porpoises broke the surface and gracefully rolled back underwater. It was like having front-row seats to our own personal marine show.

After the ceremony Mom took Sandra back to the hotel, but my dad went with me to the reception. Dad had taken eight years to finish high school because he'd alternated years between working on the farm and attending classes, so he had never considered himself an educated man. Yet he was social and completely comfortable mingling at the reception with a room full of dignitaries.

As CO, Commander Mariner wasted no time expanding the duties of our aggressor squadron. She lobbied for increased funding so we could fly more missions, and she molded our squadron into a well-oiled machine. I was busier than I had ever been in my life, and I was having the time of my life.

One crisp fall morning in 1990, I was assigned a mission to simulate a Silkworm missile attack on one of our ships off the coast of Southern California, south of some of the Channel Islands. I would be flying a two-seat A-7 with Lisa Nowak in my back seat. Lisa was a naval flight officer, and she would operate the jamming pods and radar during the mission. She also was one of the nicest, not to mention one of the most brilliant, people I had ever met.

The Silkworm was a Chinese-made missile designed to fly low across the surface of the ocean to avoid radar detection. As it got close, it would pop up and come straight down on its target. Lisa and I were trying to simulate this profile as closely as possible. We also increased the element of surprise by approaching the ship from behind an island to ensure that the ship's radar didn't detect us. We launched from Point Mugu and headed out low over the Pacific to our initial point about twenty miles from the ship.

One of my favorite things to do in the A-7 was low-level flying. Up at altitude, you have no real sense of how fast you are going, but down low is a different story. Traveling at five hundred miles an hour some two hundred feet above the ground—or water—is a serious rush. The world races by, and there is little room for error.

On our first run we made our approach from the north. Just as we got to the island, I pulled up and started a steep climb to simulate the Silkworm profile. I tried to give the ship as much altitude as I could while maintaining tactical airspeed so they could practice acquiring and tracking us with their radar. At somewhere around fifteen thousand feet, I rolled over and pulled the nose down to point right at the ship.

Our target that day was a guided missile destroyer, which, while not as big as an aircraft carrier, was a big ship. I kept my nose on it in about a 50-degree dive until it seemed to fill my windscreen, then pulled up into another steep climb. Just as I started to pull off, I noticed a huge splash right beside the ship. As we climbed out of the exercise, I did a victory roll. It just seemed like the right thing to do. (I admit: I did it because it was fun!) Lisa calmly reminded me that aerobatics weren't allowed over the ship. I made a mental note. I guess I had missed that in the squadron's standard operating procedures.

"By the way," Lisa said. "What do you think that splash was?"

"You saw it too?" I said. "Maybe they're practicing lowering lifeboats?"

She chuckled, and we set up for another run. I flew the same profile, but this time Lisa hit them with a different jamming problem to solve. As I was pulling off from the second run, we both saw another huge splash beside the ship. This piqued my curiosity, and I radioed the ship to ask what was causing it.

The voice on the other end laughed. "It's a whale. She's been playing beside the ship for two days now. We can't shake her!"

The whale apparently had taken a liking to the handsome, gray guided-missile destroyer. Where else could you see something like that? I loved my job. And not long after that day, I found out it was going to get even better!

Dwight and Tammie Jo, 1963

Tammie Jo and Dwight
on Honey, 1964

Tammie Jo's
prekindergarten
picture, 1965

Mom, Sandra, Dwight, Dad,
and Tammie Jo, Florida
Mesa, Colorado, 1967

Dad at High Nogal Ranch, Tularosa, New Mexico, 1974

Tammie Jo's first 4H calf, George, was a Brangus steer, 1974

Tammie Jo, Sandra, and D'Shane welcoming a new baby calf

Rascal, Tammie Jo's German shepherd, loved to run with her horse, Peanuts

Tammie Jo after her eighth grade honors banquet, Tularosa, New Mexico

D'Shane, Mom, Dad,
Sandra, Dwight, and
Tammie Jo Bonnell, 1979

Tammie Jo's high school
senior picture, 1979

MidAmerica Nazarene
College Volleyball Team, 1981
(Tammie Jo, front row left)

MidAmerica Nazarene
College Cheer Team,
Colorado Springs, following a
football game, 1982 (Tammie
Jo, third from right, was team
captain her senior year)

Tammie Jo, javelin
throw at a senior-year
track meet, 1983

Tammie Jo being sworn in to the Navy at Western New Mexico University, 1985

Tammie Jo's Aviation Officer Candidate School boot camp graduation, no smiling allowed, 1985

Tammie Jo in full flight gear, 1986

Tammie Jo in the front cockpit of an A-4 Skyhawk, flying an approach in formation, 1987

Navy flight training is complete, 1987

Tammie Jo with Bill Calvert, Air Combat Maneuvers (ACM) partner, in front of the A-4 Skyhawk

ACM instructor congratulates Tammie Jo

Flight line traditional ceremony commemorating Tammie Jo's last training flight

Tammie Jo at her official winging ceremony, April 17, 1987

Tammie Jo on the wing of an A-4 Skyhawk, 1987

Dean and Tammie Jo in a pre-wedding photo with an A-4 in the background, 1988

Tammie Jo and Dean walking through the traditional military sword arch on their wedding day, November 26, 1988

A-7 aircraft from Tammie Jo's VAQ-34 Flashback squadron, transiting to mission, 1989

Pam Lyons Carel, Tammie Jo, and ground crew, A-7 weapons detachment, El Centro, California, 1989

A-3 Whale with two A-7 Corsairs in formation, 1989

Tammie Jo, Sue Hart,
and Linda Heid Maloney
on detachment,
Puerto Rico, 1992

Dean and Tammie Jo
in front of a freshly
painted F/A-18
Hornet, VFA-27, 1991

CRACKDOWN ON ENLISTED WARFARE QUALIFICATIONS

NAVY TIMES
The Independent Newspaper Serving Navy, Marine Corps and Coast Guard People

42nd YEAR, No. 31   May 10, 1993 $2.00

TAILHOOK:
WHAT THE
INVESTIGATION
REALLY COST

CLINTON'S HEALTH PLAN WOULD DO AWAY WITH CHAMPUS

VAQ-34 counts 7 women
among its 13 aviators

INTO COMBAT
The only question is when

© Army Times Publishing Co.   Postmaster: Please forward if change due to official orders, see DMM sec 159.223

248786

Brenda Scheufele, Tammie Jo, and Pam Lyons Carel,
Navy Times, May 10, 1993

Family flight, with Dean
in the pilot's seat

The family's first
backpacking camping
trip, Enchanted Rock,
Fredericksburg,
Texas, 2000

Sydney, Dean, and
Marshall on a hunting
trip (while avoiding
alligators), south of
San Antonio, 2006

Tammie Jo, Marshall,
Sydney, and Dean
on a family ski trip,
Snowbird, Utah, 2005

Tammie Jo, Sydney, Dean, and Marshall, 2006

Sydney, Tammie Jo, and Marshall at a family ski vacation, Brighton, Utah, 2007

Sydney, Tammie Jo, and Marshall, 2007

Superhero Theme Night, T Bar M, New Braunfels, Texas, August 2010

Marshall and Sydney, 2015
(Marshall is smiling only
because he's holding a
popsicle on Sydney's back;
she never flinched.)

Dean, Tammie Jo, and Marshall,
Aztec, New Mexico, 2016

Tammie Jo and Marshall at
javelin practice, prep for
Texas Relays, March 2017

Tammie Jo, Riley Cantrell, Lexi
Kinchen, and Tracey Kinchen,
before Riley heads to college,
Cibolo Creek Ranch, Texas, 2017

The VAQ Girls: Tammie Jo, Pam Lyons Carel, Rosemary Mariner, Sue Hart, Brenda Scheufele, and Linda Heid Maloney, Boerne, Texas, May 25, 2005

Kandy Johnson Hintor, Jasmine Pagan, Sydney, and Tammie Jo in her Cessna 177 RG Cardinal, summer 2017

Captain Rosemary Mariner, Tammie Jo, and Captain Tommy Mariner; Rosemary's induction into the Women in Aviation Hall of Fame, summer 2017

Dean and Lexi Lou, the Shults's adopted axis deer, December 2017

Tammie Jo and her mom, December 2017

The world as seen through Sandra's eyes

View of the damaged engine, cowling, and wing from the galley door of Flight 1380

View of the exposed engine from Flight 1380; pieces of the cowling were found below the flight path

Captain Tammie Jo Shults and First Officer Chris Hall, May 16, 2018 (her first flight after Flight 1380)

Seanique Mallory, Kathryn Sandoval, Darren Ellisor, Tammie Jo, and Rachel Fernheimer, Flight 1380 crew, just prior to *CBS Morning Show* interview, May 23, 2018

Footsteps Bible study group, April 30, 2018

Tammie Jo and her Hill Country Comets javelin throwers, May 2018

Morning tea with the gang: Little Bit (white-tail deer rescued by Sydney), Critter the cat, and Sadie Mae the Brittany spaniel, June 2018

CHAPTER 9

THE FERRARI
OF THE SKIES

People who say, "It can't be done," should not
interrupt those who are doing it.
—*PUCK* MAGAZINE

Commander Mariner sensed a change was coming. Rumors circulated that the combat exclusion policy would be lifted soon, and she was one of the drivers behind that change. While I was still at VAQ-34, she made it possible for a few of us to obtain our A-7 weapons qualifications.

I think she did this for a couple of reasons. On a personal

level, it helped us prepare to transition into a fleet squadron if and when it opened up. On a grander scale, she was demonstrating to those who would decide whether to change the policy that it was not only feasible; it had already been done.

So I returned to VA-122 in Lemoore to complete weapons training. I was going to get to bomb and strafe! There I met Pam Lyons, who was in VA-122 as a student on her way to joining us in VAQ-34.

Dean was gone on detachment when I first arrived, but after he returned, for the first time in nearly two years, we saw each other on more than weekends. We reveled in the more traditional arrangement of living in the same house. It was a novelty, and I loved it. Little by little Dean and I made our house our home. I decorated and sewed curtains, and he built a handsome deck out back with seating around it. We hosted a squadron party. Our retired neighbors, Tom and Edna Dowd, checked in daily. Many days I woke up and simply thought, *I am so blessed.*

But VA-122 hadn't changed. After completing the two-week ground school portion of our weapons training, and before we did our bombing and strafing exercises in El Centro, Pam and I were scheduled for a nighttime warm-up flight. We headed out in a three-plane formation with Pam in one A-7, me in another, and an instructor in the lead.

We had briefed to fly cruise formation out to the practice area, so Pam and I would be flying behind and slightly higher than our lead, with one of us on each wing. Tighter safety rules govern night flights, but in a surprise move that defied these, our instructor descended toward the high mountains of the Sierra Nevadas, then rolled his plane upside down before descending the other side of the ridgeline.

The instructor was trying to shake us off his wing—or worse.

The move was dangerous, and he must have known it. This "dust-off" maneuver simply was not done. A flight lead is supposed to be just that: the lead. The person in that position is supposed to be watching out for his wingmen and flying like he intends to return with them. A core value of flying formation is "flight integrity," which means watching out for each other.

We were flying in a loose cruise formation, Pam on one side and me on the other, above the lead. To remain in position, Pam and I would have had to hold our position above his wings when he rolled over, a move that would have put us between him and the ground. Flying upside down is not a big deal in tactical aviation. But you would never put your wingmen upside down and close to the ground, especially at night. You'd never expect them to fly formation and ground avoidance at the same time. Our instructor had put us in a risky situation. It simply wasn't done, day or night.

The leadership of the squadron had already made it clear that Pam and I were not welcome. For example, when Pam received mail, the XO would throw it across the hangar. If she wanted it, she had to go gather it up off the floor. The enlisted troops saw what was happening and started holding back her mail so that they could hand it to her.

In spite of our lead's dangerous move, our job was to follow him. We refused to be brushed off and instinctively pulled in closer and transitioned to a safer position under his wing, keeping him between us and the mountainside.

He descended the slope halfway down into a valley before rolling upright again.

The whole experience felt a little contrived. His disregard for Pam and me—his wingmen—made me think of Black Socks's behavior on my partial-panel flight. While flying upside down, I wondered if our instructor had made a bet with his buddies that he could lose us.

After we landed, we all returned to the ready room. The other pilots were obviously surprised to see Pam and me with the instructor. At best, their squadron fun would have shamed us if we lost our place on his wing and had to fly back without him, "single ship." At worst . . . well, I try to give them the benefit of the doubt by believing they didn't wish for that.

Of course, we were still in a season when few female naval pilots and even fewer female tactical aircraft pilots existed. Some male pilots welcomed us and others didn't. As I had experienced during my first round in VA-122, the men who seemed most annoyed by our presence were those who, I suspect, attached their sense of identity to being an attack pilot. They didn't want girls playing in their sandbox. I tried to win those guys over the way I had when Nelson and his buddies came over for supper and birthday cake or when I managed to change Captain Cornejo's opinion that women shouldn't be in the cockpit, but it didn't always work.

The A-7 weapons detachment proved a hard nut to crack. Pam and I did well in strafing and bombing, so well that the officer in charge seemed to resent our performance. He decided independently that female pilots wouldn't be allowed to do strafing runs with bullets, even though the male pilots used bullets and our skipper had paid for us to do the same. He also made the call to put female pilots in a different flight with a truncated syllabus that he made up day to day. Our bombing flights might also get the cut, he told us. We were to learn nothing new, defeating the whole point of our doing the weapons training.

It was a frustrating environment. It took a couple of phone calls to ensure our funded weapons training continued—with weapons involved.

Some of the guys were pulling for Pam and me, not necessarily from the cockpit but from the hangar—the enlisted troops. One day our flight instructor said a lot of negative things about having to fly with "the girls" on a bombing flight. He beat Pam and me down to maintenance and selected the A-7 with the tightest bombing pattern. I suspect the master chief who was assigning aircraft might have noticed and mentioned the childish behavior to his troops on the flight line.

Once in his jet, the instructor couldn't see the guys on the ground checking his bombs. Pam and I, in jets on either side of him on the tarmac, could. As I looked over, I saw one guy using a huge pair of pliers to bend the bombs' fins, twisting them at odd angles. When I thought of the implications, all I could do was laugh.

I had my helmet on, and my oxygen mask was hanging to the side. I radioed Pam. "Go Barbie," I said. This was our code for switching to a private frequency: 333.3.

"Check out Sweetie's bombs," I told her. Sweetie was our nickname for him, not his actual call sign.

We both could hardly finish our checklists, we were laughing so hard.

As the three of us taxied out, the ground crew lined up, big grins on their faces, and did the wave like a football stadium cheer. That day our instructor didn't get a single bomb on target. He wasn't even close.

We had to fly with Sweetie for several sorties. Perhaps I should say *he* had to fly with *us*. The general attitude of the instructors was a little surly toward us in front of the ground crew. And, strangely enough, they often slung bombs all over Southern California but nowhere near the bull's-eye. They called it "the curse of the girls."

During this time, a congressional committee came through Lemoore. We female aviators never even saw the visitors. I assumed they spoke with the squadron commanders. Around the same time a female reporter made a visit and took a quick flight in a two-seater F/A-18 Hornet, and, I believe, she might have been taken up in an A-7 as well. She declared that no woman could handle the physical strain of piloting such aircraft. It was impossible, she said. She was adamant that women could not operate in such an intense and dynamic environment.

I could only shake my head in disbelief. She hadn't spent eight years and a thousand hours training for the experience. She hadn't been to boot camp. She hadn't spent time in a simulator or been to ground school or started out flying in the smaller planes. She hadn't been tested and shaped over time by mentoring or the force of sheer willpower that it took to succeed in this job. But there she was, taking a vehement stand against something she knew nothing about. Who knew how many people might read her article and think it was authoritative?

Those of us who were doing the "impossible" just shook our heads and realized how easy it is for anyone with a microphone to say anything they like.

In the end, while we were not allowed by the officer in charge to do the same syllabus as the men, Pam and I did do some bombing and strafing components in the A-7. Some ladies, such as Lori Melling, went on to be test pilots and flew dozens of aircraft and weapons systems. I think Pam and I were the first women to go on an A-7 weapons detachment since Commander Mariner, who had done so about a decade earlier.

We finished our weapons training, and we finished well. Commander Mariner considered this a good warm-up and signed us up to keep going. (If you're first into the jungle, you need a good machete to cut a path. Pam and I didn't have a machete; we *were* the machete.) The coolest jet in the Navy's inventory at that time was the F/A-18 Hornet, but there were no opportunities for women to fly them. I don't remember the exact conversation that took place—or where it even happened, whether a list was posted to a wall or the news came to us during a regular Monday morning officers' briefing. I do recall there was no grand fanfare involved, and that was by design. Commander Mariner wanted to keep things as quiet as possible. She blocked media access to us and said no on our behalf to all interviews. She knew the decision that had been made would stir up a hornet's nest—so to speak. But the bottom line was incredible news.

Pam and I had been selected to go to VFA-125, the F/A-18's RAG. We were going to fly Hornets!

*   *   *

It's hard to fully describe a Hornet to someone who has never seen one up close. It's the type of aircraft you want to get your picture taken next to when you're at an airshow. The Blue Angels fly Hornets. They are incredible machines—fast, agile twin-engine fighters and attack jets with a top speed of Mach 1.8, well beyond the speed of sound. They combine fighter agility and speed with a stable air-to-ground weapons-delivery platform—two functions in one package advanced enough to do it all from a single seat.

As always, Hornet training started with ground school, and then we advanced to flying the simulator. When I finally sat in an actual Hornet cockpit for my first flight, the jet seemed as tough from the cockpit looking out as it had from the ground looking up. The throttles and stick were covered with buttons and switches, which allowed the pilot to do everything from fire missiles to designate targets on a cockpit computer screen without letting go. The edge of the cockpit was nearly as low as my elbows, and the canopy formed a glass bubble over the top. The visibility ahead and behind was incredible.

No experience on the ground came close to flying an F/A-18. I was flying the Ferrari of the skies, and it felt better than riding the fastest horse I've ever been on while running belly-low in an all-out sprint. The real beauty wasn't in the Hornet's speed but in its maneuverability. The aircraft handled intuitively. I could look in any direction, and it seemed the plane would fly that way.

Later, when I first flew in formation, it seemed that the lead Hornet couldn't hold still. His wings appeared to be constantly in motion, the effect of a new generation of aircraft and software. It was truly a dream to fly. I loved the challenge of organizing and taming a thousand details into a tight economy of mind and motion. The Hornet was as graceful as it was lethal.

My initial instructor for the Hornet, Mike Frische (call sign Micro), was a superb pilot and a genuine gentleman. Flying with him felt like flying with an older brother. My very first flight in the jet was a cross-country flight to Chicago, and it was surreal to be flying what I had always admired but never dreamed of getting to fly. In a nutshell: it was a blast.

Unfortunately no one followed Micro's class act for quite some time. Squadron leadership continued to chafe at the presence of female pilots. The skipper avoided eye contact with me. On an even higher level, the commanding officer of the base chewed me out after one of my troops took a picture of me in front of an F/A-18 and the photo appeared in the *Navy Times*. In the image, the wind was blowing my regulation-length hair to the side. Standing in his office at attention, I was verbally disciplined for having hair that was "too thick."

★　★　★

The operations officer at the time (I'll call him Ziffel) was tall and a bit stout, in his early thirties. He was set to give Pam an instrument checkride, but when she had a schedule conflict, we switched flights and instructors. As I briefed with Ziffel, I could tell by the set of his jaw and his lack of eye contact that he didn't want me there. Sure enough, as soon as we finished the simulator session, he launched into a tirade.

"Women should not be in the squadron!" Ziffel said. "Only warriors deserve to fly this plane." While it was true I hadn't been to war, neither had he, so I thought he used the term with a little more weight than he deserved to.

He continued his rant. When he wasn't looking, I glanced at my watch. I needed to get to the squadron and set up the board to brief a four-plane formation flight. I was the lead, and time was ticking, but the Ops O stayed on his soapbox. When he finally paused, I told him I needed to get to my next brief. But he didn't stop. For a long while I held my tongue. By the time another pause came, I'd had enough.

"Sir," I said, "you have the right to feel the way you do. But I would say the solution is to convey your displeasure to your congressman. Vote in such a manner that your voice is heard. By law I have the right to wear this uniform, and, quite frankly, I need to get on with my next brief."

This annoyed the Ops O, but I was persistent. He had to fill out my grade sheet while I was present, so he eventually scowled and scrawled his way through the form. He found an area where he could give me one "below average" mark, then scribbled his signature and thrust the form at me. I took it and ran to my brief, making it just in time.

That night my phone rang at home. Dean was flying on detachment somewhere, so I answered, thinking it might be him. But the Ops O's voice thundered across the line. It was slightly slurred, and I suspected he had been drinking. He spoke intensely about his hatred for me.

"I'm not going to pass you," he announced. "Women have no right to be here!" I listened for a while, but when I could hear his drinking buddies cheering him on in the background, I hung up.

The call upset me, but my parents' words of wisdom came to mind: "Consider the source." In times like these it was important to take stock of my own motives for flying, for sticking with it in spite of the opposition. Had I given Ziffel any reason to have such loathing for me? Did I have the skills I needed to be in the program? Was I here on real merit? The milestones I had passed and the evaluations in my training jacket—the folder that held records of my flight performance—said I was.

What were my motives for being there? Was I there for the applause? Nope—there was none. I was there because I loved my country and wanted to serve. I also wanted to earn a living because I had more than my own home to care about. I wanted the means to take care of my sister, my parents, and even my brothers, who time and again had helped me. That's what families do. And, of course, I wanted to *fly*.

I had a family that cherished me and a faith that assured me there were no second-class citizens, that we each have the same innate, inalienable dignity and right to try. I realized I had certain skills, and my worth was determined by my Maker, not my instructor. This was the truth I needed on days when people like Ziffel sent me a different message.

The next morning I figured that after the Ops O sobered up, his tone might change. But when I reached the base and went to the training department to pick up my training jacket, I found he'd put a long, handwritten letter inside. It went on for pages, every line a hurried scrawl. According to the letter, I was "a terrible pilot" and "a terrible person." Training jackets can include only Navy-approved forms, but this letter was written on yellow loose-leaf, legal-size paper. I wasn't sure what to do with it.

Commander Mariner had moved on from VAQ-34 by then. She'd earned a master's degree in national security strategy from the National War College and was writing high-level speeches for the chiefs of staff in Washington, DC. I called her and asked for advice.

"He probably just got stirred up when his buddies were around," she said. "Take your jacket privately to his office, remind him that only approved forms are allowed, and say you'd appreciate him removing the letter. He'll do it because it doesn't behoove him to break policy like this." She always looked at the better side of humanity.

When I went back to the training department to get the jacket, it had mysteriously disappeared. I visited the Ops O without it.

In his office Ziffel scowled in my general direction but wouldn't look me in the eye. I asked him to remove the letter from my jacket, then added: "If you want to vent about my being here, you can go up the chain of command. But my jacket needs to be about flying only."

He harrumphed and said, "I need to make a phone call. You can leave."

After I did my next flight and needed to put another form in the training jacket, I learned it was still missing. I managed to continue with that day's flights, but the next day it still hadn't turned up. This went on for a few days until the officer in charge of the training department pulled me aside and said, "Lieutenant

Shults, I'm sorry, but we're going to have to stop your training until we can find your jacket."

I took a deep breath and said, "Don't worry. I'll track it down." I marched over to the Ops O's office and asked him where was my jacket.

"Don't bother me," he said. "I'm busy."

The squadron stopped my training for a week or so while the jacket was mysteriously missing.

I called Commander Mariner again. She suggested I present the problem to the JAG officer (naval attorney). Apparently she also mentioned the issue to someone else because the next day I was called into the XO's office, and he let me have it.

"How dare you go outside the squadron to talk with anyone!" the XO shouted at me. I assumed he and Ziffel were good friends. "You had no right to call your old skipper! You will not call her again!"

I stood at attention and appreciated the military bearing I'd learned in AOCS while the drill instructor shouted us down. I knew how to be emotionless on the outside, free to think as I wished on the inside.

Not surprisingly, my training jacket mysteriously reappeared the next day. My training resumed although I was required to redo my instrument checkride with a different instructor. Ziffel simply "could not grade it."

In those seasons that seemed so bleak, with forces set against me while Dean was away on detachments or cruises, I often called my parents. My mother would answer the phone with practical cheeriness in her voice. She would listen to my laments, agree with my sentiments, then often say the same thing: "Life may look hard right now, Tammie Jo, but tomorrow morning the sun will rise and the birds will sing. The people who are against you don't hold the order of your life in their hands. God is in control of that. And don't take any of their accusations too personally. Jesus was perfect, yet He was treated far worse. So, take heart, hon. When you struggle, you're in good company."

Daddy had different advice, but I would have been in trouble if I'd put his candid thoughts into action.

*   *   *

Early one morning, after spending the previous evening with friends who had a baby girl, Dean laid his head on my stomach while we were still in bed and wondered aloud when we were going to have a baby of our own. I also wanted a baby, yet as we talked about it, we didn't come up with a clear answer regarding timing.

We often discussed our plans for the future and where we might be sent when the next set of orders came through. Military life is uncertain that way. My career was exciting, but I didn't want to raise a family in a situation where Dean and I weren't living in the same place even when our squadrons were both home. A promotion in the Navy often means more time away from home. And while some people have formed amazing families and raised great kids doing it this way, it just wasn't what I wanted. I had several years of flying ahead of me, but I was nearing the end of my eight-year Navy commitment, which meant a crossroads lay ahead. Would I seek something new? Dean and I had a couple of years to think about it, so in the meantime we poured ourselves into our marriage, our jobs at our squadrons, our roles and relationships at Lakeside Community Church, and our friendships.

When I finished my F/A-18 training, I returned to VAQ-34

and resumed flying aggressor missions, now in the Hornet. I continued to make simulated attacks on ships, but now I was a far more dynamic target because the Hornet had afterburners, something the A-7 didn't have. We also took on more air-to-air missions as bogies for TOPGUN as well as other squadrons. At other times we were basically "grapes," flying in straight lines or perhaps making a turn or two just to complicate the radar picture. But even when we weren't pulling g's, we were still flying Hornets. I knew this opportunity wouldn't last forever, and I wanted to make the most of it.

I focused on flying the F/A-18 and enjoyed serving with my troops in AV/ARM, the largest division, which included three shops—electronics, avionics, and armament—with about sixty enlisted troops. They worked hard, and I loved helping them succeed inside as well as outside the Navy.

I thoroughly enjoyed working with Pam (Lyons) Carel and a couple of other women who were flying the Hornet then, Sue (Hart) Lilly and Brenda Scheufele. Pam, Sue, and I all turned thirty at about the same time, so we spent a four-day birthday-celebration weekend in Southern California "doing LA." We stayed on the *Queen Mary* and visited the *Spruce Goose*, among other attractions. Some of our back seaters, including Linda (Heid) Maloney (VAQ-33), Lisa Nowak, and Sally Fountain, were equally amazing on the ground and in the air. There was no posturing for position among us, no "alpha Barbie tactics," just hard work and meaningful friendships inside and outside of the aircraft.

In the summer of 1991, VAQ-34 moved from Point Mugu up and inland to Lemoore. While this was a huge upheaval to most, when I heard the news, I inwardly skipped all the way back to my office. Dean and I would be living in the same town! Detachments and cruises would still happen, but we would keep our parachute bags (Navy equivalent of a suitcase) in the same house. This was going to be fun.

One day later that year I woke up, had breakfast with Dean, gave him a kiss, and headed over to the base. After getting the weather and some other mission information, the division gathered for a brief; then I headed downstairs to the paraloft to gear up. I always enjoyed bantering with the para riggers as I suited up. I said hi to the guys, put on my g-suit and torso harness, and slipped on my SV2 survival-gear vest. Then I grabbed my helmet and headed out to fly. The weather was crisp, which meant the aircraft would perform even better than usual.

In the morning, before the jet engines start up, the flight line has a rich silence. I climbed into the cockpit and settled in, then put my helmet on. A feeling of seclusion and peacefulness came over me. No one was talking over the radio just then, and I had time to think through the flight and the nuances that perhaps hadn't been covered in the brief. I loved this quiet time of anticipation.

When the plane captain cleared the area, I could see rather than hear the other three aircraft start up as I fired up my own engines. Even with my helmet on, the sound filled a familiar void. That rumble always kicked the speed and attentiveness of my mind up a notch.

Today was my turn to lead a division. A thrill ran through me as I copied down my clearance. It was incredible that this was just another day at the office. Flying the Hornet never got old. This assignment, though not a fleet squadron, wasn't a bad way to serve.

★ ★ ★

I arrived at my career crossroads in early 1993. I had stayed a year beyond my commitment to the Navy, and I sensed my time in the military was drawing to a close. VAQ-34 was standing down and starting to be dismantled. The military offered me a number of other positions, including the chance to go to graduate school. While these were great offers, I had reached a point in my career where transitioning to a fleet squadron was not an option, and the other jobs that were offered were not compatible with the vision I had for my family life with kids. Dean and I both made the decision to step into civilian life, one of us at a time. Dean would do a two-year tour instructing at the Strike Fighter Weapons School Pacific while I transitioned into civilian life.

I finished my official tour of duty in March 1993. Sue Hart was getting out the same day, and we did our final flight as a section in single-seat Hornets. (Pam Lyons stayed on and became the first female naval aviator to fly in combat.) When Sue and I went out, we didn't have a mission to accomplish, so we simply briefed what we planned to do and where we wanted to go. When we were about thirty miles offshore, we started with a supersonic barrel roll. Beyond that, you need special clearance to know those details. For this ride we had two-thousand-pound fuel tanks but no pods (the containers that house the jamming radar and simulation radar), so we went fast and far.

When we were finished, I grabbed a pen and piece of paper while I sat in the hot pits (where pilots can refuel without shutting down the aircraft). I placed my hands above the canopy railing so the ground crew could see I wouldn't be operating anything while they were underneath or near the wings. Using the glareshield as a writing surface, I wrote a note of thanks for the time I had been granted to serve my country. The note wasn't to anyone in particular—in my mind I was talking to my husband, my family and friends, and my heavenly Father. I was simply grateful to be born in a country I was proud to serve, one that had opened so many doors to women during my short time in the military. I sensed even more would open in the near future. The note, which I could have sent to so many people, rested for years in the pocket of the flight jacket I was wearing that day.

For two more years I continued to serve in the United States Naval Reserve in a nonflying status. By the time I left the Navy for good in 1995, I'd become a lieutenant commander and had received a National Defense Service Medal and an expert pistol marksmanship medal and twice received the Navy and Marine Corps Achievement Medal. I thought back to the reporter who had declared women unfit to fly jets and wondered, *Who were you to make that kind of declaration for all women?*

I wouldn't trade my years in the military for anything. I learned and developed some valuable flying and leadership skills and enjoyed some tremendous friendships with both men and women, and, in the end, I succeeded. Becoming a military pilot is a highly competitive career path. It isn't easy, but it is worth it.

Do I think of myself as a trailblazer? No. It's true that I made a small mark in history, along with Pam, in the first class to have female pilots flying the F/A-18, but I don't think of myself as any sort of pioneer. My intent was not to change the military but simply to fly in it. Only after finishing certain phases of flight training or flying certain aircraft did I realize, *Wow. I guess we did something that hasn't been done before.* Not every "first" is celebrated with a ticker-tape parade.

Commander Mariner and her classmates unlocked doors and forged paths for those of us who followed her. I would like to think the women of my generation cleared some paths and helped level the playing field for the ladies who followed us in the ensuing years. Motive and merit matter, especially when you open doors for the first time.

It is rare that one person in time can change the course of history, be that in aviation or the military or any other arena. I owe the opportunities I received in aviation to a host of people, beginning with the men who unlocked those doors as well as the women ahead of me who pushed them open. If the admirals hadn't supported us, if the Commander Mariners hadn't championed us, if the Micros hadn't welcomed us, if the enlisted servicemen and servicewomen hadn't given us a hand . . . we would not have succeeded.

CHAPTER 10

I AM NOT YOUR FRIEND

The greater the difficulty, the more glory in surmounting it.
Skillful pilots gain their reputation from storms and tempests.

—EPICTETUS

A s my military career was winding down, an F/A-18 simulator instructor I knew asked if I'd be interested in firefighting. Forest fires, that is. Every summer he worked for a company called Serve Air, which contracted with the state of California to fight fires from the skies. He was ready to hand off his baton, and because Serve Air encouraged its pilots to find their own replacements, he offered his job to me. Dean was still in the Navy, and I didn't have anything in particular on the schedule that summer, so I accepted, then flew to Santa Rosa, California, to train in the Cessna O-2 Skymaster.

Apart from a few flying lessons after I graduated from college, this was my first time flying a piston-engine aircraft. It was a twin-engine plane, but the engines were in the front and the back rather than out on the wings. I had to learn about the care and feeding of piston engines, which was new to me, having come from a background of flying turbine engines in the Navy.

My new job was called "the air attack position," which meant I was tasked with spotting fires, reconnaissance, and keeping an eye out for the people on the ground. The Skymaster was certainly no Hornet, but I enjoyed the challenges of flying low and slow in the mountains, as well as the camaraderie of my new "squadron."

Flying for Serve Air was a bit how I imagined old-fashioned barnstorming to be. The aircraft themselves were old, mostly military surplus. They'd been pulled out of mothballs from the Davis-Monthan Air Force Base in Tucson, Arizona, affectionately known as the boneyards. The larger planes—the S-2s and P-2s—carried a heavy red-mud retardant that both smothered fires and contained a fertilizer to encourage new growth afterward. The Cessna I flew had seen time in Vietnam, and bullet holes still "vented" the fuselage. Although my plane bore battle scars, it ran like a top with new, more powerful Continental engines and updated avionics, including a GPS.

I flew over fires with a forest ranger sitting beside me. In military terms, we were the forward air controllers, directing a coordinated ground and air assault on our enemy—the fire. The ranger primarily focused his attention on the firefighters on the ground while I managed the air attack. We flew in ahead of the bombers to get the lay of the land. We gathered data about wind speed and direction as well as temperatures at different altitudes over the fire. We also had to determine the location of firefighters on the ground and if there were any man-made structures in the area. With all of that information, we would identify the best direction for the bombers to approach and drop their mud on the fire.

Like moths to a flame, news helicopters would inevitably arrive on the scene. If they pressed in too close, it was my job to steer them clear of the paths of the aircraft laying down retardant. When the drops started in earnest, the activity often reminded me of flying the gunnery pattern in the T-2. Multiple aircraft circled in a daisy chain, dropping into the canyons one after the other, much like we'd done in our jets when we rolled in off a high perch to attack the banner. In both cases there were lots of airplanes in a small piece of sky. When done right, it was poetry in motion. Otherwise, it was an accident waiting to happen.

Late one afternoon, the ranger and I circled over a raging fire being chased by the wind up multiple canyons. Firefighters on top of a ridgeline were surrounded on three sides by the blaze. The wind changed direction, and we could see fingers of fire creeping up the hill behind them, threatening to cut off their only escape route. They needed to evacuate *now*.

I flew in low over the group, and the ranger threw out a large weighted bag attached to a long red streamer, a signal alerting them to retreat immediately. Their escape route was drawn on a map inside the pouch. In case they couldn't get to it, I circled back around and flew over them in the only direction they could go to safety. I made one last pass to make sure they got the message.

They did, and fortunately they all survived. Some days we saved more than architecture and landscapes. We were able to fly between disaster and those brave hearts on the ground who put their lives on the line every time they showed up.

Later in the season, law-enforcement officials investigated a rash of fires and concluded they were the work of a lone arsonist who was staying a step ahead of them by listening to their radio transmissions. I was tasked with flying encrypted radios to different locations around the state so the good guys could communicate without the arsonist listening in. It worked. They caught him, and the fires stopped.

"Well, dang it all anyway," quipped one of the older pilots. "We just put ourselves out of work!"

Another pilot jokingly set out a tip jar to raise money for the arsonist's bail. We ended up using the money to buy groceries instead. Having to scramble to be airborne within ten minutes of any call meant we couldn't go out to eat, so we grilled a lot. Those guys were masters at cooking just about anything you can imagine on a barbecue pit. Grilled pizza was my all-time favorite.

Just as the season was drawing to a close, a large fire broke out in a populated area of Riverside County, and we were called back into action. We moved our base of operations to Hemet, California, and fought the fire into November, well after the fire season had officially ended. Apparently forest fires have no respect for their official season.

My birthday falls in early November, so on that evening the other pilots invited me out "to go drinking," as they put it.

"Thanks," I said. "I'd love to, but I don't drink."

One of the guys piped up, "That's okay. We'll drink *for* you!"

Off we marched to the nearest watering hole. Most of the pilots were closer to my father's age than mine, and they spent the evening regaling me with funny stories until my eyes ran with tears and my sides ached. It was a most memorable birthday.

That season of firefighting turned out to be a great transition into civilian life for me. The flying was like something out of the Wild West with seemingly no rules. Everyone knew their mission as well as their aircraft, and they were willing to do whatever it took to get the job done. All summer long I was in awe as I circled overhead and watched them dive into smoke-filled canyons and selflessly put themselves in harm's way for the sake of protecting others. Flying with this group renewed my love of aviation, and to this day I am both honored and humbled that they accepted me into their ranks and counted me as one of their own.

When we weren't out looking for or battling fires, often we were hanging around the fire station telling stories. Mainly, I listened. That group of aviators, including one other woman, had remarkable histories in aviation, and yet they were some of the humblest pilots I had ever met. A number of them had served in Vietnam, and a few had flown in the 1989 movie *Always*, about aerial firefighters. Those guys liked to joke about how their incredible aviation prowess had finally been captured on film. They were all accomplished aviators doing some of the most demanding flying in aviation, and there was not even a hint of competition among them. They all seemed comfortable in their own skin, having nothing to prove and unthreatened by the others at the table. It was refreshing, and I loved every minute of it.

My short time with Serve Air was a joy, but when the Hemet fire was finally under control, it was time to go home and look to the future. As much as I enjoyed it, I knew fighting forest fires was not going to last. Dean and I would be moving as soon as his latest tour in the Navy ended. I wasn't really sure what my next step in life would be. Very little hiring was going on in the airline industry, and I was in a bit of a life pause. We wanted children, but none had shown up to date. Then, out of the blue, an opportunity appeared on the horizon.

*   *   *

The local churches in Lemoore were having a ladies' luncheon, and the coordinators invited me to come and share my story. After I spoke, one of the women there introduced herself and told me that if I was considering flying for the airlines, I should talk to her son, Steve Martin, who was a pilot with Southwest Airlines. A few days later Steve called me. He encouraged me to apply to Southwest and said he'd be happy to help. He also let me know that I'd have to move quickly because Southwest accepted pilot applications only once a year, and I'd need to have a 737-type rating before I could apply. Southwest was the only airline that required their incoming pilots to have this rating.

This started the wheels turning in my mind. Though Dean and I had plans to start a family, it was impossible to say when that would happen, and the thought of hanging around the house waiting for the day I would become a mom seemed counterproductive. Dean was on a detachment to Australia when I spoke to Steve, so I was full of news when he called home one evening. I told him what I'd learned about applying at Southwest.

We agreed I would get my 737-type rating and apply. Fortunately the GI Bill paid the $9,000 fee required to take the course and get the rating. As I look back now, I appreciate how much Dean encouraged me to pursue this new venture. In fact, we both had wanted to work for Southwest. With him on board, I got busy and began the process of becoming a commercial airline pilot.

Obtaining a 737-type rating was no easy matter in the early 1990s. Just finding a seat in one of the few schools in the country that offered the training was a challenge. The military was facing budget cuts after the First Gulf War and was offering severance packages to encourage pilots to leave the service, so there was a glut of pilots on the market, all vying for a limited number of jobs in commercial aviation. Many of those pilots were pursuing their 737-type rating in hopes of landing a job with Southwest, just as I was.

Fortunately, I found a school in Los Angeles that had a slot available on short notice. This turned out to be a good-news, bad-news story. The good news was I would obtain the rating in time to apply to Southwest during their next application period. The bad news was the school was run by a group of men from a part of the world where women were not allowed to drive, much less fly airplanes. Needless to say, they held little, if any, respect for women.

After ground school in Los Angeles, I went with my class to Phoenix for the simulator phase of our training. When that phase ended, we were to go back to Los Angeles for our checkrides. When the Phoenix simulator developed a mechanical problem, the company arranged to take my class back to Los Angeles early to finish up—and they left me behind!

I made this discovery the next day in my hotel lobby after everyone was gone. When I called the school and asked why this had happened, I was told, "You don't need the checkride. You are a woman and don't need a job."

They scheduled men from two classes behind me for check-rides while I waited. I couldn't believe it. After a great introduction to civilian aviation with Serve Air, I thought I had seen the last of that mind-set when I left the military. But this attitude seemed to be rooted in a different culture's even stronger bias.

"Well," I said, "I've paid the fee for that checkride, so if you won't let me do it, I'll need my money back." Fortunately, it didn't come to that, and I eventually headed back home with my 737-type rating in hand.

Southwest was the only commercial airline I was interested in flying for. I had done some homework and learned that Southwest was a financially solid company that valued their employees as well as their customers. People seemed to love working for the "Luv Airline." As a pilot, I found Southwest appealing because they flew only 737s, which had a two-man cockpit. Other airlines flew planes with three-man cockpits, which included a flight engineer who did not fly. With Southwest I would get to fly the first day on the line rather than "sitting sideways" for years as a flight engineer and working my way up to first officer. Southwest also had bases in Texas, which is where Dean and I wanted to live eventually. It seemed like the perfect fit.

I wasn't the only pilot who realized the benefits of flying for Southwest, so the competition was fierce. Steve wasn't kidding when he told me the opportunity to turn in my application would come and go quickly. When Southwest opened the window, they accepted the first five thousand applications, then closed the window until the following year. You could mail your application, but if it was postmarked before opening day, it would be rejected. And if it wasn't one of the first five thousand received after the window opened, it would end up in the trash then too. Having an employee hand deliver your application to the People Department (as they called human resources) and put in a good word for you was a plus.

The year I applied, Southwest received more than five thousand applications on the first day! If I recall correctly, they were planning to hire two hundred pilots from that pool. Fortunately I had help getting my application into the right hands that day, and it wasn't long before I received a call from Southwest inviting me to interview. When they called, they asked if I knew of any other female pilots with similar military experience. My friend Sue Hart was the only one I could think of who'd left the Navy, and she'd landed a job with FedEx. I'm not sure if that made me a rare breed or an odd duck.

I flew out to Phoenix for an interview, and a few weeks later I was offered a job. I would start training in March 1994. The six-week training program at Southwest was both exciting and overwhelming. I was one of two female pilots in a class of twenty; the other was Cathy Dees. The pilots trained in the same building as the flight attendants. In that day their classes were predominately female, and the pilot classes were overwhelmingly male (less than 3 percent of Southwest pilots were women). It wasn't unusual for Cathy and me to be mistaken for flight attendants in the halls of the training center. We took that as a compliment.

Southwest's corporate culture was, and still is, legendary. It has been studied and written about in business schools across the nation, and countless companies have tried to emulate the culture that cofounder Herb Kelleher created. When I joined Southwest he was chairman, president, and CEO, and he led his company with a servant's heart. "If you take care of your people, they will take care of your customers," he often said, and he always lived by that belief.

In the early 1990s, Southwest was a David competing against the Goliaths of the airline industry, and Herb was a master at rallying the troops to take on the giants. Everyone, including

Herb, was on a first-name basis, and once he met an employee, he never forgot their name. He led by example in working harder than the competition, and he seemed to have a lot of fun doing it. By Herb's design, Southwest was supposed to be a fun place to work. In spite of this noble goal, several factors threatened to undermine it.

In general, airlines around the country were changing the way they operated. As new methods of teamwork that focused on the crew were introduced, the change was embraced by many but fiercely resisted by some captains who had long ruled as kings without a Magna Carta.

In addition, the overall climate of the commercial airline industry in the early 1990s was still rather chilly toward female pilots, and Southwest wasn't insulated from those attitudes. Though women had been flying for the company for about ten years, we were still few, and the good-ol'-boy network was still alive and well. I would soon find out that some of those men weren't excited about having more women in their ranks, particularly one who had the audacity to have flown a jet with afterburners.

Recent events had raised their hackles. Just three years earlier, a scandal had surrounded the Tailhook Convention of 1991. Tailhook, as it was known, was an annual gathering in Las Vegas of Navy and Marine Corps aviators. While it afforded an opportunity for junior officers to meet and mingle with the upper echelons of Navy officers, it also had the reputation for being a breeding ground for ungentlemanly behavior. In 1991 a female naval aviator had accused a number of her male peers of sexual assault, and the accusation had been found to have merit. The Department of the Navy launched an investigation that resulted in the formal discipline of fourteen admirals and some three hundred naval aviators, and the secretary of defense had issued a report that mandated change. (That convention took place the first time Dean and I were both home together. We'd considered attending, but fortunately opted to go backpacking in the Sierra Nevadas instead.)

Some insiders felt the discipline was unfair because all men who attended were caught up in the controversy. Others agreed that it was time for change and that the housecleaning was long overdue. The incident reminded me of the conversation we had at our family dinner table about bullies: "If you see an injustice and do nothing to stop it," my parents had said, "you're part of the problem. Silence is consent." Regardless of where one stood on the issue, there was no denying that the fallout from Tailhook was far-reaching.

Then in 1994, just months after I began at Southwest, naval aviator Kara Hultgreen died behind the boat during a carrier landing in her F-14 Tomcat. She was one of the first women qualified to fly in a combat squadron. While making an approach to USS *Abraham Lincoln*, Kara experienced a compressor stall in the left engine and was unable to recover the aircraft. When the crew ejected, the radar-intercept officer (RIO) in the back seat went first. He survived. She did not.

Kara died serving her country in one of the most dangerous environments in all of aviation, just as many men had before her. But that didn't stop some people from using this to support their arguments that women didn't belong in the cockpit and certainly not in fighters. For some time her tragic death and the Tailhook scandal cropped up in nearly every cockpit conversation, usually in the form of a soapbox monologue that labeled women unfit for the rigors of aviation.

Fortunately, in my early days at Southwest, the majority of captains I flew with had great attitudes. One of my very first captains, Sumner Wyall, was legendary within the Southwest pilot ranks. I think I heard my first Sumner story before I even finished training, so I was happy to see my name on the flight schedule with his. On our first day of flying together, I noticed he wore a pair of silver aviator wings that had been crafted into a ring. When I asked about it, he told me the wings had belonged to his mother, who'd flown with the Women's Airforce Service Pilots (WASPs) during World War II. She had taught him to fly.

Sumner was funny and lighthearted and had a contagious laugh. Other captains I flew with early on were just as pleasant, often darting off between flights and returning with treats for their new first officer. How could I not feel welcomed?

★　★　★

After I finished training and completed a few assigned trips, I got my first "hard line" assignment. That meant I would fly for one month with the same captain. I was on the schedule at last!

I'll call the captain I was first paired with Captain Henry. I would find out later that this man was a classic bully, and nobody, man or woman, liked flying with him. It's a wonder he wanted to fly for Southwest because he exhibited the exact antithesis of the company's attitude.

Captain Henry didn't talk to me; he yelled. *Loud* was his only volume. Once, after we landed and pulled into the gate, he opened the cockpit door and launched into a tirade. He was so vocal that a flight attendant shut the door, fearing passengers would be alarmed.

In another instance he wouldn't allow me to configure the landing gear and flaps in time to make a landing on the first approach, then became furious with me when we had to circle around and try again.

On yet another occasion he shoved a checklist in front of my face and held it there while I was trying to land. In his estimation I was the worst pilot he'd ever flown with. He bragged that he knew exactly what he was doing, adding that he'd flown F-14s in the Navy. I thought we might find some common ground and started to say that I, too, had flown jets in the Navy, but he cut me off and said, "I don't care what you flew or where!"

The captain had an unusual landing technique in which he rotated the yoke side to side and up and down in a "wipeout" of the controls just before touchdown. This maneuver made the aircraft wobble slightly just before touching down, often resulting in a pretty firm landing. After one particularly interesting landing in Las Vegas, we pulled into the gate, and he opened the door as passengers were leaving. One glared into the cockpit on his way by and said, "That was the craziest landing I've ever experienced. It was *the girl*, wasn't it?"

"Yep!" Captain Henry nodded.

The man couldn't pass up any chance to land an insult, even if it wasn't true.

Having had to deal with a few men of his caliber in the Navy, I had some experience in handling the hard cases, so I tried to find some common ground outside of flying before I gave up on him. Despite my best efforts, however, I had no luck. After our first full trip together, I began to wonder if I'd made a grave mistake in becoming an airline pilot.

I got home and unloaded on Dean; then I told Steve Martin about my experience with Captain Henry. Steve had become a friend, and I asked for his advice. He assured me that the captain's behavior was not the norm at Southwest and advised me to give away all of my trips with him to other pilots, then pick up flights with other captains. New pilots have a lot to learn when they first get on the line, and in Steve's opinion, I wasn't going to learn anything worthwhile from Captain Henry. I took Steve's advice and ended up flying with some refreshingly professional men who took the time to teach me what I needed to know about flying "on the line" at Southwest. It *was* a dream job.

Interestingly, about a year later, the company hired an outside party to assess the main reasons pilots called in sick. They concluded that first officers having to fly with certain captains was a major recurring issue. This prompted Southwest to institute a new program called avoidance bidding, in which first officers can discreetly avoid flying with particular captains.

Sadly, that program wasn't even on the horizon when I was hired, and the very next month I drew the short straw again. Captain Henry behaved even worse than he had on our last trip together. I had never experienced anything like it. He was beyond unprofessional, so I took the advice of another pilot and went to Professional Standards, a group within Southwest designed to help resolve conflict before it escalates up the chain of command. That didn't work, and I was called in for a team meeting with the chief pilot, a Professional Standards representative, and Captain Henry himself. They asked why I'd put my flights up for giveaway. When I explained that the captain and I weren't able to communicate, Captain Henry came out of the corner swinging. At one point he said, "I hate communicating with her because she reminds me of my wife. And I hate communicating with my wife."

At that, the chief pilot turned to me and said, "Tammie Jo, you're free to leave the meeting." The Professional Standards representative followed me out and thanked me for keeping my cool. While I felt relieved that the chief pilot seemed to understand my concerns, I was disappointed when Captain Henry was allowed to keep flying with no consequences even though he had admitted to his unprofessional behavior.

That was my first experience with the good-ol'-boy network in my new flight department. It wouldn't be my last. I started to hear ripples of gossip that put me in an unflattering light, to put it mildly. It seemed Captain Henry was telling anyone who would listen about his "horrific" experience with me, and he did most of his storytelling after hours at the bar, where untruths often morph into legends.

I decided I wouldn't allow myself to be provoked. I had survived similar attacks in the Navy by taking the same approach. I vented my frustrations in my journal, then closed the book and pressed on. The months went by smoothly, and I flew with some terrific captains. Occasionally they'd joke about "girl pilots," and I would always toss the jokes back.

One day an older captain met me in the jetway before we started that day. "Hmm. Another empty kitchen," he said, meaning that since I was here flying with him, somewhere a kitchen didn't have a woman in it.

I looked him over and shot back, "Hmm. Another empty golf cart."

We eyed each other for a moment, then laughed. I came to realize that flying with a woman was out of the ordinary for a lot of guys. A few of them told me they'd never flown with a woman. So sometimes they would say things to test the waters. When they saw I could roll with the punches and even return a few, we would get along fine. That kind of thing didn't bother me. I have two brothers. I know the game.

Other pilots behaved in ways that were just as inappropriate as Captain Henry had been, if less aggressive. For one month I flew with a guy I'll call Captain Hugh. His reputation preceded him because he told anybody who'd listen about his sexual escapades. During our first flight, after we reached altitude, he turned the conversation to sex. I switched the conversation back to flying. The next day the same thing happened. Once we were airborne, his talk quickly turned to sex. This went on all month long, and all month long I simply refused to get drawn into this inappropriate topic. His lack of professionalism still shocks me. At the end of the month, he gave me a lousy probation review. This didn't surprise me. I only wished he had been honest in his critique, which should have read, "First Officer Shults repeatedly refused to discuss sex with me; therefore, I believe she is a bad pilot."

Probation at Southwest lasts for one year. Every captain a probationary pilot flies with writes a critique of his or her flying ability, attitude, and professional appearance. By the time my probation ended, all my critiques were above average except those from Captain Henry, Captain Hugh, and a third man who outdid them both.

★   ★   ★

In spite of these outlier experiences, as a company, Southwest lived up to the reputation that had first attracted me. Overall, the airline was positive and proactive, and, for the most part, so were its employees. I met terrific people.

I flew with Jim Rice, a senior check airman, incredible aviator, and gentleman in every way. I flew with Dave "Fig" Newton, one of those big-brained aeronautical-engineer types who does much more than just fly for the company. I still enjoy his sense of humor. Fig has Herb Kelleher's gift of making people feel valued. Whenever I flew with him, I felt like one of the gang. I flew with Scott Brewster, another brilliant man and fantastic aviator. I can't say enough good about Scott. I flew with Nancy Bruce, a lady who knows more about 737 systems than anyone I've ever met. Jim Seydewitz, Todd Kloss, and Wally Cox are also exceptional aviators as well as charming people. From them I learned much more than how to fly a 737. I learned what it means to be a great captain.

No organization, however, is immune to humans who sometimes make poor decisions or people who wield their authority in harmful ways. I met the man I'll call Captain Janus for the first time in the pilots' lounge, and he seemed friendly enough in front of the other pilots. We walked to the aircraft together, did all the checklists, and soon took off. Once the engines are running, pilots observe a sterile-cockpit rule, meaning we don't speak about anything but flight-related items until after the plane reaches ten thousand feet.

When we reached ten thousand feet on that first flight, Captain Janus turned to me, pointed his finger in my face, and said, "I hate you. I am not your friend. I don't want to hear anything from you unless I ask for a checklist."

Because he'd been so nice in the pilots' lounge, I thought he might be joking. Maybe he'd break into a grin or start cracking up. He did not. I held my tongue and said nothing but what the checklists required. After we landed, he was lighthearted with the flight attendants, even a little flirty. The Dr. Jekyll and Mr. Hyde act was jaw-dropping. I swiftly reverted to the military bearing I'd learned in AOCS, revealing nothing outwardly, silently pledging to find some common ground.

On future flights I spoke to Captain Janus when we were

above ten thousand feet, trying to find a subject we could both enjoy. We would be spending a lot of hours side by side, and I refused to believe his initial statements were the sum total of his personality. I wanted to get along with this man, or the month would be miserable for us both.

This time I determined not to change my schedule or put any of my trips up for giveaway. I wouldn't take anything personally. I wouldn't sink to his level. But it didn't take long to see this guy had his cap set against me, and he found bizarre ways to be spiteful.

At the end of our third flight together, he extended my release papers to me and asked, "Want these?"

"Yes, thank you," I said, reaching for them.

He crumpled the papers, threw them in the trash, and poured his coffee over them. I retrieved the pages, dried them with a paper towel, and tried to make them readable. When we finished the next flight and the operations agent brought in the new set of paperwork, he did the same thing: ask, crumple, pour. He did this on every single flight we took together.

For. The. Whole. Month.

Once, between flights, he disappeared. I presumed he'd gone to get something to eat. While he was away, I helped the flight attendants pick up trash and cross seatbelts. We talked for a little while. I had found that mingling with the cabin crew and lending a hand helped me keep my perspective. While I was doing this, Captain Janus returned to the cockpit. He pulled my pilot's hat off the clip where I'd stowed it, threw it on the floor, and stomped on it.

The hat was ruined. A new hat cost sixty dollars. It was a required part of my uniform, so I bought a new hat. The next trip, he stomped on my new one, destroying it as well. I bought two new hats before I got wise and started keeping it out of his sight.

By the end of my first year with Southwest, I had flown with more than forty different captains. Almost all forty filled out their forms about me professionally, gave me above-average grades, and had nothing bad to say. Captains Henry, Hugh, and Janus, however, were condescending and hypercritical.

Rather than use the standard form, Captain Janus typed his one-sentence report on a blank piece of paper: "There were such differences between her and me that I can't even critique her." I was called into the assistant chief pilot's office to explain.

"What's this about?" the assistant chief pilot asked, showing me the page.

I was three weeks away from getting off probation. I was tired of the drama, and I didn't want another meeting in which a hateful colleague was allowed to vent. So I said, "It's over. I'd rather not talk about it."

"I don't think you understand," he said. "I'm your assistant chief, and I'm not asking. I'm telling you to explain what went on in the cockpit. It's Southwest's business to know."

So I told him about the month I'd flown with Captain Janus. First I recounted the things he'd done that were safety concerns, then I repeated the things he'd said to me. I mentioned the cups of coffee he'd poured on my releases and the hats he'd stomped. Once a week he had told me to gather my things: "You're being replaced," he'd say. Fortunately I'd never abandoned my post, but he'd done his best to get rid of me.

When I finished, the assistant chief instructed me to put what I'd told him in writing. I told him I just wanted to move on. I didn't have any desire to recount that month on paper.

"I am your boss, and I said I want it in writing," he said. I would like to think the assistant chief wasn't trying to put me in a bad spot. "You won't be allowed to fly until you give me a full report. You have a week to get it done."

I went back to my journals, where I'd recorded my experiences in detail. On every trip Captain Janus had not only insulted and harassed me; he'd routinely conducted himself as a pilot in ways that I found alarming. I tried to focus my report on these behaviors rather than on his personal incivility. Even so, it was hard to consolidate that month into anything shorter than a booklet.

The chief and assistant chief called Captain Janus in for a meeting. Later the assistant chief told me they gave him the opportunity to tell his side of the story first, which he did. Then they read my statement to him in its entirety. When they finished, they asked him if what I had written was true.

"So?" he said.

Captain Janus was reprimanded and subjected to disciplinary action, then resumed his regular job.

Thanks to the negative reports those three captains had written about me, I had to do an extra, nonstandard, three-day checkride with a check airman before I was allowed to complete my probationary checkride in the simulator. I heard later that the check airman had been briefed before our flight and was told that I was arrogant—and worse. He was a former Blue Angel, competent, composed, and professional. His report about me was also only one line: "I don't see any problems with her."

After the ensuing simulator checkride—which I passed "with flying colors" (their words, not mine)—my probationary time finally, officially ended. I started to breathe easy again. I was confident in my ability to fly the 737 and feeling good about my new job as a first officer. Having faced the bullies and survived, I believed I could successfully overcome whatever challenges might lay ahead.

Unfortunately I would soon have the opportunity to put that belief to the test.

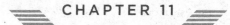

CHAPTER 11

THE TRUTH WILL OUTLIVE A LIE

*Football's important to me, but it's not my life. It's
not the biggest thing in my life. My faith is. . . .
No matter how big the situation is, it's not really
going to define me. I put my identity in who
Christ thinks I am and who I know He says I am.*
—AMERICAN QUARTERBACK TREVOR LAWRENCE

Up to that point in my career, countless situations had
reminded me that no one's opinion could define my self-
worth. One particular experience during my early years as a
Southwest pilot would test everything I'd learned.

During the year I was on probation at Southwest, I often flew out of Houston or Dallas, even though my home with Dean was in California, where he was still stationed in the Navy. It was a grueling season of commuting, hopping flights from California to Texas before beginning each trip.

After I finished my first year and achieved a few months of seniority, I was able to switch my base to Phoenix, which cut my commute in half. I was a junior pilot at this point, and I was on reserve. That meant I didn't have an assigned flight schedule, but each month I had to be in Phoenix on standby for a designated number of days, ready to fly with two hours' notice if they needed me. Most days I ended up flying.

The first time I arrived in Phoenix, I went to introduce myself to the chief pilot and his assistant. This is customary when flying out of a new base. The chief wasn't in, but his assistant chief was, so I knocked on the door. He called me in.

The first thing I noticed in his office was an enormous painting on the wall behind him. It was of an F-15 Eagle, the reigning fighter in the US Air Force at the time. Clearly he had flown the Eagle, and this was his baby. A friendly competition exists between Eagle pilots and Hornet pilots, and I was fairly certain the assistant chief knew my background because we were a small airline. I didn't make a big deal over the aircraft I'd flown, however, and I seldom told people about my experiences in the Hornet unless they asked or the topic was pertinent.

When I entered his office, he left me standing while he slouched behind his desk. Rather than return my greeting, he launched into a lecture. Nobody cared what I'd flown in the military, he said. We were all Boeing pilots here. Nobody wanted to hear about the Hornet, and it was in my best interest to keep my head down and my mouth shut.

I remained quiet and soaked in this odd welcome.

"So you think you're special," he eventually said.

I was still wondering why he'd felt the lecture was necessary and had no idea where he was going. "No, sir. I don't."

"You don't think there's *anything* different about you?"

"No, sir."

He repeated, "You don't think you're different at all?"

I tried to smile politely and said, "I guess I am a little different. In a bushel of red apples, I'm a green apple, but I'm still just an apple."

At that, the assistant chief resumed his lecture. "We're all just pilots here," he repeated. "Your past is just that—your past. No one cares."

It was hard not to compliment the desk-sized testament to his past taking up the wall behind him. But I kept my mouth shut. When he finished and I said nothing, he shook his head and pointed toward the door. On that strange note, I left to fly my next trip.

What had triggered this chilly reception? I sure didn't know. I decided not to dwell on it and concentrated instead on my job.

A few weeks after I started flying out of Phoenix, I was summoned to the chief pilot's office. This time the chief was there with the assistant chief. Neither of them smiled or invited me to sit.

The chief said, "Have you ever damaged an aircraft?"

"No, sir."

He asked the question again in a slightly different way.

Again I said, "No, sir."

Tag-teaming, the two of them began to shoot off rapid-fire queries that dealt with every conceivable part of an aircraft. Had I ever put excess wear and tear on an aircraft? Had I ever damaged a tire? Had I ever cracked a windshield? Had I ever scuffed the paint?

My answer was always "No, sir"—with the exception of confirming I'd experienced some flat and blown tires.

Abruptly the assistant chief opened the door and pointed for me to leave. I asked what the questions were about, but they both stayed as silent as stone.

A week later I was called in to another meeting. This time a union representative I'll call Captain Arnold joined me. His presence surprised me. I hadn't asked for a representative. Why would I need one?

Captain Arnold met me in the hallway and didn't introduce himself. He only said, "What have you screwed up now?"

I was taken aback. "I have no idea what you're talking about," I said.

"Yes you do," he said. He headed into the chief's office, and I followed him, totally confused.

This meeting was almost an exact repeat of the first. The three men drilled me with the same line of questioning. Again they went over every part of a plane. Again they offered no explanation about why they were asking these questions. Interestingly my union rep stayed on the chief pilot's side of the questioning. The notion of a union rep was new to me; of course we didn't have a union in the military. But he didn't come across to me the way I felt an advocate should, and when the meeting was over, I wasn't sure I even wanted a rep.

When the meeting ended, Captain Arnold showed me out.

Within a week a friend in headquarters called me and said in a hushed voice, "Tammie Jo, I have no idea what's going on, but they just pulled your application and went over it with a fine-tooth comb. Some of the ladies in Phoenix said they're trying to claim you lied on your application, that you don't really have a clean safety record."

Stunned, I thanked my friend and hung up. They were questioning my safety record? I'd received my first 1,000-hour safety award back when I'd finished flying the A-7 Corsairs at Point Mugu, and I'd achieved every safety-standard award possible in my naval career. Some kind of trouble was brewing, but I couldn't imagine what it was.

Once again I turned to my trusted mentor and called Rosemary Mariner, who was a captain at the time, for advice. She suggested I get an attorney. I didn't want to do that. Not yet. All my flight records were in order. I would ask the union to defend me if I needed to. Until then I tried to keep things as low-key as possible.

The matter did not stay low-key. I learned that Captain Arnold was close friends with the chief and his assistant. He was on their side, not mine. So I called the union and spoke with someone else, Captain Len Legge. He checked around and suspected something underhanded was going on. Though it wasn't a simple thing to change union reps, he promised to see what he could do for me.

Little by little I drew back the curtain on this strange story. A pilot who'd recently been hired by Southwest as a first officer was a former naval aviator. He saw me from a distance one day walking across the ramp and casually remarked to his captain: "I know that girl from the Navy. She crashed an A-7 once. I don't feel safe with her here." That captain escorted this man to the chief pilot and the assistant chief to spill this "news."

The "crash" the first officer referred to was the Black Socks episode in which my flight instruments failed, my instructor abandoned me on approach in a storm, and I slid off the runway. Thanks to then-Commander Mariner, an independent team of investigators found "no pilot error." I'd had a mechanical failure accompanied by a flight-lead failure. End of story. The incident had not been credited to me, so it had no bearing on my safety record.

Had they been interested in the truth, the chief and assistant chief could have asked to see my training jacket from the Navy, which showed a perfect safety record. They could have seen my logbooks, which are officially annotated and stamped if any accident or incident occurs. They could have called Captain Mariner, my commanding officer at the time, and asked her to explain the situation. They could have requested a copy of my naval safety record, which confirmed the Navy's findings of "no pilot error." Yet when I offered all these documents to the chiefs, they refused to look at them. Instead, they called a number of people from VA-122 to ask for their accounts of the incident. Though many of these statements conflicted and were not officially recognized, the chiefs looked no further.

They summoned me to their office again. This time the chief pilot accused me of lying on my application. I'd checked the box indicating I had no accidents, and he believed I didn't have a clean safety record. He fired me and told me to surrender my ID badge immediately.

I asked them to look at my Navy records before they finalized the decision.

The chief said, "We have no interest in your records."

These guys weren't just snakes that could be taken care of with a Coke bottle. They were bullies, and bullies are always cowards. Gossip that supported their purpose was good enough for them. I couldn't present my records. I couldn't face my accuser. It just didn't add up to a legitimate inquiry.

At the union office Captain Legge kept notes of what had

happened. He assured me that this story wasn't over yet. It seemed pretty well over to me. Since Dean was away for new-hire training at Southwest, I went to my parents' home in New Mexico. My parents had been with me every step along the way of my career, and they were as crushed as I was.

Again I called Captain Mariner, who pointed me toward some attorneys she knew who had experience with situations like mine. I didn't call them right away. I'd been leveled by the chiefs' first hard punch.

*   *   *

Stress washed over me like a tsunami. A union article that dragged my name through the mud had been printed after my unfortunate experience with Captain Janus, so this firing seemed to lend credence to the article's claims.

My humiliation was profound. I talked to a few people I trusted, but nobody seemed quite sure how to advise me. For weeks my head throbbed constantly, and my stomach ached. I would open my Bible and read, mostly from the Old Testament, just to remember that not every story is fair, but there is still goodness in life. I had problems sleeping. One of my front teeth turned gray, and my doctor said the discoloration was caused by stress. More than once I broke down crying and found it nearly impossible to stop. I didn't go anywhere. Often I found myself home alone.

This was an incredibly hard time, but it wasn't without purpose. I was surrounded by the love of friends and family who reminded me daily of who I was apart from my career.

Dean helped me keep my sanity. He had recently exited the military, and we'd moved from California to Bandera, Texas, by this point. It was impossible for him to avoid all the juicy gossip about the Navy Hornet pilot who'd gotten fired while he was in the new-hire training. Because Southwest Airlines is a first-name-basis company, not everyone realized they were talking in front of him about his wife. But he stayed above the fray, which was a gift to me. As our sole breadwinner now, he needed to keep working. We never really questioned whether Dean would keep flying for the airline because we believed my firing was the decision of two renegade men and not a systemic corporate problem.

The rest of my family, my parents and siblings, simply wrapped their arms around me. They couldn't fight the battle for me, but they helped tend my wounds.

My path through this season didn't lead straight out. I had to land on my knees when I got out of bed in the mornings, if I got up at all. When you're depressed, it's hard to see in the dark without friends to guide you through. The pianist from church, a rancher's wife named Pat Welch, would call in the mornings until I answered the phone and assured her I was up and facing the day. Kandy Johnson and Arlene Fender, friends from my college days, took time off work and flew from Kansas City to Bandera to encourage me in person. We were able to laugh a bit together, and they helped me see that, yes, I could have a life beyond the aviation industry.

Our dearest neighbors, Betty Brister and Marshall Patton, had me over for coffee every day. Marshall, from Oklahoma, was a college football player turned professional rodeo bulldogger who had eventually become an entrepreneur in the oil industry. He was also a tongue-in-cheek proponent of dueling. Once during this melee, he remarked to me that people would be more cautious with their words if they had to physically answer for them.

Though it wasn't charitable of me, I couldn't help but agree with him. After all, I had a height advantage over both chiefs—maybe that would give me an edge. At least it gave me a smile.

During those months, I spent a lot of time reading the Psalms. I found these words of King David particularly helpful:

> Contend, LORD, with those who contend with me;
>> fight against those who fight against me.
> Take up shield and armor;
>> arise and come to my aid. . . .
> Say to me,
>> "I am your salvation." (Psalm 35:1–3 NIV)

One morning when I woke, God cleared my head. *All right*, I sensed Him say. *No more tears. Time to fight.* I couldn't wallow in disappointment any longer. If I did, I'd be in danger of getting wrapped up in bitterness and resentment. I knew how to fight—after all, I'd studied and was trained in tactics. I just had to decide that what I'd learned wasn't only for the military world I'd left behind.

I also knew what to do when a door to what I wanted closed in my face. I had to keep walking around the building, knocking on other doors, just as I'd done seeking entrance to the military. If none of those doors opened, I could be confident I'd done all I could, and God would see to the rest. My Confidant had my back. He knew what I needed even better than I knew myself.

I soon met with Susan Barnes and Susan Kudla, Denver-based attorneys who were in Phoenix for a conference. After they heard my story, they said they'd take my case pro bono. They asked me what I wanted most at that point. Did I want to sue the union and airline and walk away with money, or did I want my job back? Without hesitation I answered that I wanted my job back. I wanted to be left alone to fly.

My attorneys went to work. First they approached the head of my union and said, essentially, "Look, she's a member of your union. She's been wrongly accused and fired with the aid of one of your own reps. What do you want to do about this to help her, and how can we help you? Because if she can't get her job back, then we need to address your representative's failure to defend her before we address the airline."

Their approach set the union in motion. None of us ever heard from Captain Arnold again, but the astute Captain Legge took over the preparation for my defense.

I can count on one hand the people at Southwest who were brave enough to speak to me during this time. My parents pointed out that not everyone gets to see the other side of friendship's fabric. Abandonment does hurt. But it made more room in my life for true friendships. And it confirmed, once more, that I couldn't let my identity get wrapped up in being a Southwest pilot or in being a pilot of any kind. That status was obviously subject to the will of others. I was still a person of worth regardless of my title or occupation. While I don't wish this misery on anyone, an experience like mine will separate who you are from what you do.

E-mails and phone calls flew in earnest for some time. Captain Legge asked the chief pilot for permission to present the documentation that exonerated me, my safety record, and the request was denied. The case was closed, and my firing was final. Captain Legge reasoned in a subsequent letter, "We have information pertinent to this matter that has not been seen. May we submit this information?"

"No, you may not," came the reply.

Fortunately Southwest Airlines, just like the Navy, has rules for fair play. The chiefs who fired me were midlevel managers, and the company had a responsibility to delegate authority to them and trust their judgment. I understood that. But individuals don't always represent the whole, and their malevolent denial of the truth was a personal choice, not a company practice. In due process and thanks to Captain Legge's persistence, I was granted a hearing in front of four company representatives so I could present my case. The union chose two of the four members of the jury; Southwest chose the other two. All four were pilots.

During this time, Captain Nancy Bruce became my champion if ever there was one. Without her I wouldn't have known how to navigate this corporate world of who is connected to whom. Nancy prayed with me, listened to me, and helped me shine a light on the facts rather than the emotions. She helped me sort out my thoughts and avoid the black holes that would suck up my time and energy. In addition to the legal team who came to my aid—Susan Barnes and Susan Kudla, along with a Dallas-based attorney—I owe Nancy my job.

I gathered all my supporting documents. Captain Mariner flew out from Washington, DC, to testify on my behalf. I asked Captain Tom Vaughn, who'd been the skipper of Dean's squadron in Lemoore and was familiar with the Black Socks incident, for a written statement in my defense. When he heard the details of my situation, he said, "No, I won't write you a letter. I'm going to fly in and testify in person. This is important, and the truth needs to be told."

On the day of the hearing, about twenty people gathered in front of the panel of four jurors. Southwest brought its legal counsel. The vice presidents of flight operations and legal were present as well. The chief pilots who had fired me came as did the people supporting me. The first officer who had originally accused me of crashing an A-7 was conspicuously absent. Another Navy pilot agreed to testify against me, however. He'd been a lieutenant commander in VAQ-34. He had written and submitted his report before the hearing. When he was asked to testify, he simply said, "Everything is in my report. I don't have anything further to add."

Captain Legge picked up the lieutenant commander's report. "Okay," he said. "Let's go over your report statement by statement because your former commanding officer is here today. Captain Mariner was your commanding officer at the time, as well as Lieutenant Shults's, and she is familiar with all the details of the situation."

Captain Legge read the report one accusation at a time. In front of the whole room, the lieutenant commander recanted every accusation he had brought against me. Captain Mariner never had to say a word.

The hearing was supposed to last for one day. It dragged on for two. One of the four jurors was a female first officer chosen by Southwest. I didn't know her, but she proved to have the biggest ax to grind. I wondered if she was trying to show the company she wasn't going to be soft on me simply because we were both women. I never knew exactly what was behind her stance, and she continued to express animosity toward me for years after this hearing, stirring up conversations about me with other captains and even making peculiar phone calls to my husband. It seemed she was digging for personal information about me and my mental health. Dean stopped taking her calls.

At the end of the testimonies, the jury of four had to make a decision: Should I get my job back or not? When it was over, they agreed I had not lied on my application. I was a safe pilot and had always been a safe pilot. They immediately gave me my job back.

I was exhausted. At that point, six months after I'd been fired, I had some dark thoughts about what they could do with that job. But the wisdom I found in the Bible and my mom's many lessons on ladylike behavior wisely sealed my lips.

★　★　★

The vindication was rewarding at first, but in the coming days it began to feel hollow. Company officials didn't provide me with lost wages or even a formal apology, although they did give me a few days to consider whether I wanted to return. After all this turmoil, I'd won, but now I wasn't sure I wanted to claim the victory.

At home my mind churned. The stress had taken its toll on me and my family, and we all felt as if we'd been put through a meat grinder. My personal and professional reputation had been publicly smeared. I hadn't just been dragged through mud but through manure. Though I'd been exonerated, people held long memories of accusations even though they were false. Above all, I still couldn't explain why the chiefs had targeted me in the first place. It seemed I was just on the wrong side of their good-ol'-boys network. How could I know it wouldn't happen again?

Do I really want that job back? I wondered. *Do I really want to fly for Southwest?*

It was Captain Mariner who helped me answer the question. She called one day to see how I was doing and whether I'd made a decision. I told her why I was wavering.

"Either way you choose, you won't be happy for a while," she said, "not at home and not at work."

She was right. If I went back to work, I'd still have to deal with people who didn't like me, people who enjoyed spreading tantalizing gossip. If I stayed home, I'd truly miss the joy of flying.

She continued. "Some decisions we need to make aren't a matter of happiness. Ask yourself this: When you look down the road five to ten years from now and imagine yourself looking back, what will be the decision you hope you would have made? The truth will outlive a lie, Tammie Jo. It may take a while, even a long while, but truth will win in the end. And the people who don't like you don't get to determine your happiness."

Our conversation changed the way I thought about the choices in front of me.

I kept thinking. Dean and I would start a family someday and continue to live a happy life whether I took my old job back or not. That was a consolation. As a couple, the two of us were so much more than what we did for a living.

I considered my parents. Dad would be retiring soon from his work as a diesel mechanic, and I wanted to do my part for Sandra. Her health was deteriorating, and I loved her and my parents. They had done without so often to help me get through college. This job was part of what would allow me to give back. Families take care of each other; that's what families are for. Sandra had always been on the horizon as my responsibility, and someday I hoped to help my parents as well.

Flying for Southwest was a good job. I was already trained for it, and work was work, and life was life. It's nice to be able to enjoy work, but that would never be the reason why I lived and breathed.

I called Southwest and took my job back.

I picked up where I'd left off, with a small hit in my longevity status due to having been gone for six months—another injustice that was never rectified. My pay and responsibilities stayed the same. Captain Jim Rice, a hero in my eyes, arranged to fly with me on my first flight after I returned. As we boarded together, his first words to me were, "Forget about all this, Tammie Jo. Let's go fly and have some fun."

And we did. Everyone needs a Jim Rice in their life.

I saw the chief pilots who had fired me every now and again, but not often. Their practices and attitudes continued to be an issue for others. Years later I found out they had a regular practice of conducting "investigations" into their subordinates, men and women, without justifiable cause. The saying I had learned as a kid held true: bullies are never bullies to just one person. Eventually their school-bus ride came to an end, and both of them were removed from management.

The first officer, now a captain, who claimed I'd crashed an A-7 is still around today. After all these years I've never met him, but I hope he has found a healthier outlet for his time and energy. Maybe the effects of his lies about me made an impression on his moral character. I don't know. I'm only sure that we all need forgiveness.

Captain Mariner was right. The truth did outlive the lie, though the process took a long time. Five years later, at the age of thirty-nine, I upgraded to captain, a position I've held for almost two decades. And I love my company. Over the years Southwest listened, adapted, changed, and today has become one of the friendliest and most welcoming, courteous, and, in technical terms, wonderful aviation companies in the world. Not because we're perfect but because we strive to be.

When I look back now, I know I made the right choice.

CHAPTER 12

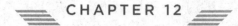

FAMILY JOYS, FAMILY TURBULENCE

The LORD is my strength and song.

—PSALM 118:14

With this battle behind us, Dean and I tried to get back into a normal routine. It wasn't easy. If you've ever cared for someone with a terrible wound, you could empathize with Dean. He was flying extra trips to help us catch up financially. On top of this, our plans to have the family we longed for became something that seemed would never happen.

201

Dean and I decided our gene pool wasn't magical, and going outside of it wouldn't be a bad idea. We began investigating adoption agencies—and they investigated us. A year later we partnered with an outreach program that provided adoption services to pregnant women needing assistance.

We reminded ourselves to be patient. And patient. And patient.

One day I got a call from Dean. I was in Las Vegas on an overnight, midtrip, and I'd gone out on a run. I slowed to a walk, my cell phone to my ear, as Dean told me about a young lady going through a divorce. She was pregnant and unable to provide for her little one on the way, and she felt that the best thing she could do was find a loving and stable home for her baby. Her parents were supporting her decision and had heard we were wanting to adopt. Were we interested in adopting her child?

I looked up at the azure sky, amazed. I was amazed at the selfless love of the young woman. Amazed at the hearts of her parents, supporting her brave decision. Amazed at how our paths had crossed. Amazed that God would bless us with a child, at last. "Thank You, God!"

Although we had four months to get ready, life began to move fast. It would be a private adoption, and we had reams of legal paperwork to complete. Dean had a standing joke whenever he and I had to sign legal paperwork. He would hold his hand over the fine print and say, "Just sign at the bottom." Usually that was good enough for me. This time, of course, we hired an attorney.

State officials inspected our house. We were fingerprinted and background checked and CPR certified. We painted the nursery, bought a car seat and a stroller, and selected a crib. Sometimes when I paused long enough, I could envision our baby. I realized life was good—and it was about to get even better.

One night when I should have been asleep, I went into the

living room without turning on the lights. The brilliant glow of a full moon shined through the west window. Our baby was coming. Our baby! I felt humbled and excited. Life on the way is *life*. Someone new was coming to change not just our home but the world we lived in.

The birth mother requested a closed adoption. She wanted the baby to be considered ours. Dean and I still marvel at this young lady's wonderful, loving approach to the whole process. Her thoughtful actions were part of a beautiful love story that we would one day tell our child. We met with her once, and she let us feel the baby kick. Oh, that tiny kick—it told us how real this all was becoming.

One evening in March 1998, Dean and I worked late to finish the nursery. I graciously offered moral support by catching a few winks on the nursery couch while he stayed up all night, but I rose early to help him complete it.

The night before our baby's due date, we got the call we'd been waiting for. I had been keeping a couple of dozen cut roses in the cool garage, ready for this occasion. I scooped them up, arranged them for this wonderful woman, and we headed to the hospital.

Twenty minutes after our baby girl was born, she was placed in our arms. Sydney was beautiful, perfect, more precious than we could describe. The birth mother handed her tiny little girl to me and said, "She needs you more than she needs me." Such selfless words still echo in my mind with a ring of gratitude as I have recalled them over the years. When her family members asked if they could see the baby, the birth mother let them look from a distance, but she didn't let them hold her. She wanted Sydney to bond with us.

From the moment Sydney first opened her bright blue eyes,

she was happy and vivacious, the darling of our hearts, clearly and absolutely a work of God. An hour after she was born, she surprised all of us, perhaps even herself, by rolling over on the hospital table—the earliest sign of her inborn athletic abilities.

I took three months off work to welcome this tiny baby, *our* baby, to the world, and during that time I felt both buoyant and weighted. Even when Sydney was quiet and sleeping on my shoulder, her health and happiness were in our care. Being a parent was the most incredible job in the world. Sometimes while she slept in her crib, I'd steal into her room, kiss her cheek, and simply watch her sleep.

Dean and I had talked about me becoming a full-time mom, and we were both open to that plan. But I also had the option to fly a reduced schedule, and the more we discussed it, the more viable that option seemed. Because the aviation industry is seniority-driven, it's difficult to take a few years away from flying, then jump back in at the bottom of the seniority list. With a reduced schedule I could fly less, have more time at home, and study to stay current.

Another factor in our decision was a few years earlier Dean had a health scare. He'd been unable to focus his eyes one day, and the event had rocked our world. After a couple of days of on-our-face prayers, the vision problem was linked to a bad sinus infection. After the infection cleared up, Dean was perfectly well again. But we realized that if anything ever happened to him, I'd need to be able to help support our family. So after those three months at home, I returned to work.

Sydney was a gregarious baby, active, moving all the time, alert and awake. She giggled. She cooed. She soon learned to roll over intentionally. She learned to blow kisses and to crawl. We marveled at each stage of growth. By the time Sydney was nine months old, she took off walking. Life became a happy whirlwind of activity and love.

When Sydney turned fourteen months old, Dean and I began the process of filling out paperwork to adopt a second child, but I started feeling unwell. I was tired. Out of gas. Nauseated. Usually I ran a four-mile loop each morning, but suddenly I could hardly walk a mile.

I had terrible thoughts of cancer. Dean was away on a trip, so I called my mom.

"Whatever it is, you're going to have to face it," she said gently. "Sooner is better than later. Take a pregnancy test."

"I'm not pregnant."

"It's the first thing a doctor will ask you, Tammie Jo. Go ahead and do that, then move on to the next logical step."

I took a home pregnancy test. I shook my head and took another test. The second test confirmed the first. I hesitantly wrote the word in my journal: *Pregnant.*

The following day Sydney and I met Dean at a hotel near the airport because he had a San Antonio overnight and needed to go out early the next morning. I planned to have a bit of fun letting him know we were pregnant and typed up a little agreement. After we checked into our room, I presented it to him with my hand over everything but the signature line.

"Just sign at the bottom," I said with a smile, handing him a pen. He hesitated, recognizing his own jesting turned back at him.

After he signed his name, I removed my hand.

Agreement #1. You will always outweigh me no matter how big I get.

Agreement #2. You will walk with me whether I want to walk or not.

Agreement #3. You will keep pickles and ice cream—or whatever crazy food I crave—well within my reach when needed.

Dean grinned as the reason for these promises dawned on him. He was so happy, he actually leaped from one hotel bed to the next and back again. Little Sydney stood under the arc of his jumps and stared at this new act.

We made a pact not to tell anyone for another month but almost didn't make it when a little boy's comment sparked a joke in the pilots' lounge. The preschooler boarded my plane one day but was too frightened to walk down the aisle to his seat, so his father let him have a peek in the cockpit. After he saw Captain Jan Johnson, the little boy caught sight of me.

"Look!" the boy told his dad. "He's flying with his mama!" The airplane had a mommy in the cockpit—that's all this little guy needed to know. He went to his seat reassured.

The next time I visited the pilots' lounge, I arrived an hour or two after Dean. Almost in unison my colleagues shouted, "Hi, Mama!" I shot eye daggers in Dean's direction, thinking he had spilled the beans. He wildly shook his head as if to say, *I didn't do it!* Then Captain Johnson, several years my senior, came into view with a twinkle in his eye.

"Ready to go flying, Mom?" he asked me. Dean was innocent.

Southwest offered a great maternity-leave policy, so I flew for only another two and a half months as a first officer; then I was on maternity leave until eight weeks after the birth. We didn't want to refer to our child as "it," so before we had a name picked out, we called the baby "our little stowaway" and "our little jump seater." I soon shortened this to "little one."

I enjoyed being home, though now I was constantly exhausted

and sick. Nothing seemed to settle my stomach during the pregnancy. Yet the sheer wonder of a life forming within me eclipsed everything else. Feeling that first flutter and kick inside me took my breath away. My heart was happy, simply happy, and I often found myself singing around the house.

When the big day arrived, my parents, down from New Mexico, took care of Sydney while Dean and I drove to the hospital, excited yet apprehensive. I had been scheduled for a C-section, and it went according to plan. Before long I could hear the baby fussing behind the drape. Although I couldn't see anything, Dean could.

I couldn't wait another second, so I finally asked him, "Well, boy or girl?"

"I can't tell!" Dean said. Not what a new mom wants to hear.

But soon the long-awaited baby was fully in view. He was perfect and tiny, and he was ours. We named him Marshall after our retired neighbor who, with his wife, Betty, had been so kind to us since the day we moved in next door. They were such dear friends. When Sydney saw Marshall for the first time through the glass of the nursery window, she pointed at her new baby brother with a grin and said, "Mine? Mine!"

Marshall was nothing like Sydney as a baby. He preferred sleeping to eating, and he talked with his big brown eyes rather than with his mouth. I stayed home past my paid maternity leave until he was four months old. I enjoyed being home with the children so much. Although, as most parents can guess, I was often exhausted, and the house was a constant wreck.

Sandra came to visit during this time. I always looked forward to her sweet countenance. Though she didn't walk well, she was always ready with a book and a welcoming lap, and she'd read the same story as many times as Sydney requested.

When Marshall was born, I was based in Houston as a senior first officer for Southwest. When I was nursing Marshall and studying for captain upgrade, Sydney sometimes discovered me up with my books in the middle of the night. She would get out of her little bed, grab her own book, and join me at the breakfast table to "study." This is one of those snapshots of life that will never fade.

I upgraded to captain before Marshall turned one year old. Having two children and a job with a few more responsibilities was a stretch for me, but everyone has their own life stressors. Like most people, I adapted.

* * *

Every six months during the eleven years we'd been married, Dean and I held a family meeting. We'd adopted the term as a joke and ran the meetings with lighthearted and cartoonish parliamentary procedures. While cheerful, these meetings were how we routinely evaluated and made adjustments to our life together. After the kids arrived, our meetings often addressed whether it was a good idea for me to continue working. I don't think I would have been able to keep flying if I'd been employed by any other airline. At Southwest it worked. When the kids were little, our meeting was simply a tea-and-cookies time. But as they grew older, they took part in the conversations too.

In those early years I flew about two days a week. With Dean's and my schedules overlapping four or five nights a month, we'd be gone from home at the same time, so we had in-home childcare for those nights.

For the first seven years our assistant pastor and his wife, Elmer and Jeannette Franks, were part-time help and full-time mentors for all four of us. Papa and Granny, as our kids came to know them, were wonderful friends to Dean and me and positive influences on all of us. After they retired, we were blessed with Aunt Staci, a family friend who was loving, fun, and wise beyond her twentysomething years. When Dean and I were both away from home, I would write a short devotional to be read to the kids at bedtime, or I'd make an I-spy photo collage.

Life took on a busy pace, and the years flew by. Our whole family was invested in our church, which in our small town was also our community. On the lax-to-strict spectrum, I suppose we tended toward the stricter side of parenting, yet we always tried to hand out our rules and discipline within the boundaries of love.

Dean and I had grown up doing chores, and as adults, we felt strongly about our kids participating in the running of the household. Even when our children were little, we made a game out of jobs like putting away the clean dishes, often while dancing to a VeggieTales tune.

We taught them early how to take care of others—chickens, goats, dogs, and, when the kids were older, miniature horses from my parents' mares. "Feed others before you feed yourself" was a rule at our house. To this day both of my children have a wonderful sense of what it means to love people and animals well. Dean and I might have encouraged this virtue, but they embraced the trait and nurtured it in themselves.

Starting at about age four, the kids did a special work project every summer. One summer we grew herbs and made pesto from the extra basil to give to the neighbors. The herb garden became a little resource for our neighborhood, and if we were gone, our friends would come by and pick whatever they needed. Another summer we made braided bread and cinnamon rolls, which we gave away. Another year the kids did pet sitting for vacationing families. In junior high school, Marshall raised laying hens and sold his fresh eggs.

Both of my kids learned how to sew. Marshall made tool belts. Sydney made lots of bandannas and a quilt. They took piano lessons and filled the house with happy sounds. During the summer we'd occasionally go see movies, but otherwise it was a "no TV" season. There was too much fun to be had outside, plenty of conversations to join, and great books to be read.

When Marshall was about five and Sydney was seven, I came home from taking Sydney to an all-day gymnastics competition on a Saturday. The next morning Dean left at 5:00 a.m. to go to work, and I was too tired to push the children to wake up and get ready for church, so I decided we'd have "home church" that day. The kids brought a pencil and paper and their Bibles to the table as I fixed breakfast. The plan was to read our Bibles together and talk about what we read. I made cantaloupe halves filled with berries and topped with whipped cream—a treat we all liked. While I made tea, I asked Marshall to take the fruit to our places while Sydney set the table.

"Look, Mama!" Marshall said happily. I turned to see what had made him so excited. He smiled at me with the cantaloupe bowls in both hands and said, "We are not in a hurry!"

I smiled, but the statement stopped me in my tracks. These sweet little lives had been entrusted to us to cherish, and Dean and I wanted them to taste life's richest moments—they couldn't do that if we were always in a hurry. I mulled over Marshall's statement and searched my heart. Our schedules had been crazy. I decided to take that in hand, and Dean agreed. We started limiting our extracurricular "life" to protect the sacred moments of being a family at home, not in a hurry.

As time progressed, although we often needed to move fast,

we worked harder to strike a balance in our schedules. I especially guarded mealtimes. We decided to hit the pause button on our schedules while eating together, relax a bit, and claim those moments to slow down and enjoy each other. I tried to always have a vase of something pretty on the table, even if it was just flowering weeds and a small candle.

* * *

Sydney was the reason we even thought of homeschooling. She was such a sponge for information and conversation. She had learned all of her magnet letters by the time she was two. We needed fuel to feed her little flame! So Dean and I homeschooled both children when they were young—four years for Sydney and two years for Marshall.

Later we moved to a town closer to the airport, where we found a school that used the same classical method we had been using. It seemed a good choice for us, so we plugged in to "regular" school. Marshall, our Captain Cautious, blossomed, but those years were the beginning of tough times for Sydney. Our Tarzan Cinderella missed being able to kick off her shoes, run around whenever she got fidgety, and munch on her baby carrots when she wanted.

Parenthood can be difficult under the best of circumstances, and if an extra challenge, such as a health concern, pops up, life can turn decidedly rough. When the kids were still young, Sydney needed to go to the hospital for a bilateral hernia operation. Overall, she came through her surgery fine, but while tending to her at the hospital, I experienced a horrible pain in my side. I wondered if I was experiencing sympathy pains, an idea I normally would have considered silly psychobabble.

Sydney reacted poorly to the medicine they gave her at first, so in the press to care for her more fully, I ignored my stomachache, even though it didn't go away. Once she was home and doing better, I went back to work, but on my first day back, my stomach hurt so bad I could hardly breathe. It turned out that my appendix had burst—three days earlier.

After my appendix was removed, I still didn't feel well. I felt like I was drowning every time I lay down. The doctors sent me home anyway, and soon I was having a hard time breathing in any position. The appendix infection had spread to my lungs, so I returned to the hospital for more surgery.

Things went from bad to worse. I struggled to recover from the procedure, and my legs, lungs, and chest were in constant pain. They put me on morphine. My kidneys quit functioning.

A doctor finally said, "Honestly, we're not sure how this is going to turn out. We're going to give you a different painkiller that will clear the morphine fog but still keep the pain manageable. You can sign legal paperwork while taking this drug, and you'll have a clear head to say goodbye to your loved ones, especially your children."

This wasn't comforting, but I had hurt for so long and struggled to take every breath. On some level I appreciated his straightforward words. Still, I couldn't imagine not getting to watch my kids grow up, and I loved the life that Dean and I had created together. I loved Dean.

I said my goodbyes before the surgery and, with God's help, opened my eyes after it. But the event marked the beginning of a nine-year slog through substantial health issues. For eight months I didn't fly, and for about three years after that, I seemed to catch every infection that drifted by. The heavy antibiotics apparently had sent my immune system into hibernation. For a few years it was difficult to bend over and put any pressure on my lungs. During this season, I also hurt my back, broke my foot, and had two knee surgeries. Over time, thankfully, I finally became healthy again. My fifties have been much better to me!

★   ★   ★

The rhythm of our lives resumed as I pressed through those years. The kids continued to grow, and we went on camping trips and holidays and attended plays and practices and games and recitals. We attended the T Bar M Family camps in New Braunfels, Texas every year, from the time Marshall was a baby until the kids were grown and making their own adventures. This annual vacation was an important time for us to have fun with each other and hit the "reset button" on our lives, focusing on what was important and having unhurried conversations. We never did get to Disneyland or Six Flags, opting instead for hiking and deep-sea fishing in Alaska, snorkeling in the Bahamas, and making numerous trips to New Mexico to see my parents, Mommy and Daddy Bopa, and Aunt Sandra.

Piano lessons were a staple for my children, as they had been for me. In time Sydney exchanged music lessons for drama and did well on the stage. She won awards in drama competition, adding a national award in Latin as a sixth grader competing against eighth graders.

Dean and I tried to raise our children to be confident and competent, able to function well both when we were around and when we weren't. Dean taught them to ride dirt bikes, to repair things around the house, and to fish and hunt. Sydney had all the first rites of passage that Marshall did. She shot her first deer before Marshall shot his. They learned how to skin and process

213

an animal so we could use the meat. When the kids were older, Dean taught Sydney to drive; then I taught Marshall.

Both Sydney and Marshall are natural athletes. In junior high Sydney ran cross-country in the mornings and played volleyball after school. Marshall started shagging (retrieving) the discus and had a good throw before he was old enough to join the track team. When he was in fifth grade, he was recruited at a junior high cross-country meet to join a team that was a runner short. He finished his first race in the middle of the pack—and this was before he'd ever run a quarter of a mile without stopping. The running bug had bitten him, and he's still running today.

The kids took some hits from their coaches when we prioritized family camp in August over whatever training they needed to do. Once, after we returned from the T Bar M, Marshall had to run a mile in the Texas heat in full football pads, cleats, and helmet, and Sydney was demoted from the varsity volleyball team to JV. I could only shake my head at these "punishments" and was proud of my children for taking such nonsense in stride. Family will be family long after the sporting events, and school, are over.

Dean coached YMCA basketball and football for Marshall, and I coached YMCA volleyball for Sydney. Doing this allowed us to spend more time with our kids and get to know all of their friends. This was one of the joys of parenting and kept us connected to our kids, their peers, and the world they were growing up in.

Marshall wanted to throw the javelin, so I coached him for a few years in high school. Instead of grabbing a milkshake together, we would grab a javelin and go throw. He wound up being much better at it than I had been and was eventually recruited to throw for the Air Force Academy.

Marshall has always been a hard worker and plotted his

course early in life. He wanted to be a pilot at three years old and never wavered. He has always been an old soul in a young body, practicing privately before ever performing publicly. He seemed to have practiced walking when we weren't looking because he surprised us all by just doing it one day. That is his way.

He got his private pilot's license in our little old Cessna and a glider rating before he left for the Air Force Academy in 2018. Ever since then he and Dean have been on a never-ending hunt for a faster airplane, mainly to see my eyes roll at the cost.

We asked him if choosing the Air Force over the Navy is how a good son rebels. He said he was bringing honor back to the family name. We let him have that round. After all, he was headed into boot camp.

★ ★ ★

Looking back, I smile when thinking about all those memories we made together as a family. They're important because they comingle with the frustrations and heartache that are also a part of parenting. My children's stories are not mine to tell. Sydney and Marshall will recount their own journeys to others in their own ways. But I would like to share an aspect of my experience as a mom who loves her kids wholeheartedly with a love that isn't dependent on their performance.

The truth is that what happens to your child happens to you. Sydney, always so attentive and helpful at home, struggled at school and faced some real challenges. As she grew, we learned more about the shadows of abandonment that can haunt children who've been adopted. Dean and I have tried to chase those shadows away with the light of truth and love. We slowed down to give her our ears to hear what the real issues were.

We have tried to walk alongside our daughter through exclusion, assault, addiction, miscarriage, and the heartbreakingly hard days between those difficult and life-changing events. I cannot say we've done it all gracefully, but Dean and I cling to Jesus with one hand and our family with the other. We know that the scars our daughter carries heal only with love. Gratitude is a good first step, and we continue to be grateful for a long list of blessings, one of which is that our Sydney survived so much, and we still have her.

Once, when Sydney and I went to lunch together, she said candidly, "I'm sorry I'm not the daughter you always wanted."

"But you are," I assured her as tears welled up in my eyes. The truth is so easy to speak. "You are the sweet daughter of my dreams, the daughter I prayed for, the daughter I love no matter what. I don't want more from you, I want more *for* you," I said.

Dean found a baby deer not long ago. She was lying abandoned in our yard. The fawn was all bones and ribs, hungry, and wobbly on her legs. We took her into our house and fed her from a bottle until she gradually became stronger. She bonded with us the first day, as hungry babies often do when fed. We named our fawn Lexi Lou. She slept outside in the yard, but during the early mornings and evenings, she would come inside and sleep on our dog's rug. As the weeks passed, she became one of the family, even touring around the table during game night. Whenever I looked at Lexi, I recalled Psalm 42:1, and I was reminded of the days when Sydney was farthest from us:

> As the deer pants for streams of water,
>> so my soul pants for you, my God. (NIV)

How I had hoped and prayed that the people who were closest

to her in those seasons would treat her with tenderness, like a wounded fawn who'd wandered into a backyard, needing to heal.

Recently Sydney invited Dean and me over for dinner. Everything was homemade. She lit a candle and had a pretty flower in a glass on the table and served us so gracefully. She is married now, and as I write this, she is expecting a little one of her own. Her story isn't over, but it's changing, and when I see my sweet girl, I see endless possibilities, a future for her. I think of those words from Jeremiah: "'For I know the plans that I have for you,' declares the LORD, 'plans for welfare and not for calamity to give you a future and a hope'" (29:11).

God didn't speak those words to me or Sydney, but they are words for us that reveal the character of the God who loves us. In my experience I have found that where there is life, there is a chance. Where there is God, there is hope. Life is good when you choose to live it.

We enjoyed a light and happy meal, a time together that felt like, perhaps at last, a vise was releasing our hearts. Our prayers for our children are not finished. They won't be, not as long as we are parents. I felt hope surge within my heart anew, as if telling me that seasons of great peace lay ahead.

Then, just when I thought life was back on course—finally—I faced my greatest challenge at work.

CHAPTER 13

THE CREW OF
FLIGHT 1380

*If you want to go fast, go alone. If you want to
go far, go together.*

—AFRICAN PROVERB

For decades I've started each day with a cup of tea and my Bible. And since my first flight I've prayed over my every day of flying. I didn't do this to be noble; it was far more self-serving than that. When I started, I had no idea whether I even had "the right stuff" to be a pilot, so it seemed to me a wise practice to ask God to guide my judgment and my airmanship. With time, practice, and some success, my confidence grew, both in flying and in prayer. Then, when I started flying for Southwest, I also started praying for my crew and passengers.

Nothing was different the morning of April 17, 2018. It was a Tuesday, 2:00 a.m., day two of a three-day trip that had started in Houston. Today we were headed from Nashville to New York City, then to Dallas. The trip had originally been assigned to Dean, but throughout our careers with Southwest, we'd often traded trips. This particular switch was so I could attend one of Marshall's track meets. Marshall was a high school senior, and I'd coached him and his peers in throwing events (discus, shot put, and javelin) for eight years. This would be my last season coaching our son. Dean would have loved to go himself, but he didn't hesitate to sacrifice what he wanted and give the trip to me.

In my Nashville hotel room, I brewed my tea and pulled my Bible closer. The verse I read that day was Colossians 3:17: "And whatever you do or say, do it as a representative of the Lord Jesus" (NLT).

Sometimes a verse hits home even before I know why. This one captured my attention the way a message written by a teacher in a special color of chalk stands out on a blackboard. It would stay with me throughout the day. *This message is important*, it seemed to say. *Pay attention.*

As I always do when I'm on the road, I texted a portion of my morning reading to Dean, Sydney, Marshall, and my folks as I prayed over each of them and whatever they might be doing that day. It is my way of loving on them from afar, from wherever I happen to be on any given day.

When my teacup was empty, the verse was tucked in my heart, and my prayer time was finished, I put on some Steven Curtis

Chapman music and got ready to go to work. By 4:00 a.m. I was in the hotel lobby, meeting my first officer, Darren Ellisor, so we could head to the airport.

* * *

I had met Darren the day before at Houston's Hobby Airport, where we started the trip. Dean and I have compared notes through our many years at Southwest and agree that we can have terrible weather, people drama, mechanical trouble, or delays, but if we have a good flying partner—be that a captain or a first officer—we have a good day. If the cabin crew has the same sunny outlook, it's a great day. When I met Darren, a native Texan and former Air Force pilot, I thought, *I'm in for some good days*.

When we arrived at the airport for the second day of our trip, Darren offered to grab us coffee. As much as I appreciated the gesture, I told him I'd get the coffee so he could get started on the many tasks that he had to do in the cockpit.

A short time later I stepped aboard the 737-700 that would take us to LaGuardia and introduced myself to the flight attendants for the day: Rachel Fernheimer, Seanique Mallory, and Kathryn Sandoval. It was going to be a great day! We put our things away, checked equipment, then stood in the forward galley with our coffees for a briefing. Darren came out of the cockpit to join us.

Commercial aviation is a team sport. When a crew gathers for a flight, all crew members' names are on the paperwork, but knowing the names is not the same as meeting the people and getting to know them. The trick is in figuring out how to turn five strangers into a team in five minutes or less.

Drawing our assigned crew members together at the beginning

of each day has become a habit for me, and now it's part of our protocol at Southwest Airlines. A flight crew often changes every day, sometimes multiple times through the day, so it takes a real effort to stop the busyness and focus for a moment on the team members. There's no formula for this, but one of the best lessons I learned at home was the art of asking questions and listening attentively to the answers. It's important to me to convey that nobody needs to worry whether something is "important enough" to tell the captain. If I take the time to look at a baby picture or listen to a personal story, the channels of communication open up. When I take the time to make my flight brief a dialogue rather than a monologue, it changes the posture of our future communications about everything, from equipment to people.

That day I learned that Rachel thought she and I had flown together once before, but neither of us was sure. Kathryn had been with Southwest for just six weeks. And Seanique had worked as a customer-service agent for a few years before becoming a flight attendant. In the short time we chatted together, it was immediately evident that the three women who would be assisting passengers in the cabin of Flight 1380 genuinely enjoyed their jobs. I was grateful to be working with such a great crew.

The first leg of our flight together that day, from Nashville to LaGuardia, was smooth—though I confess my landing at LaGuardia was a little more Navy than I would have liked. We rolled out, exited the runway, and made our way to the gate.

Usually, by the time passengers exit the plane and the crew cleans up the cabin, it's time to start boarding the next flight. That day, however, the schedule allowed us a few minutes to ourselves with no passengers on board. We all gathered in the galley and continued the conversation we had begun in Nashville.

Darren told us about his son's Cub Scout troop, which he

leads. He's also a Little League coach. He and I discovered we both had seniors in high school. Darren, who has four children, asked me what I was getting Marshall for a graduation gift, and we both joked about how hard it can be to find the right gift for a senior. Darren's graduate, his oldest daughter, got to choose the family vacation—a couple of weeks in Germany after a fun launch from New York. I was writing by hand the book of Proverbs for Marshall. (Don't feel sorry for him—Dean and I also gave him flight lessons and the opportunity to earn his pilot's license before graduation day, which he did.)

All three flight attendants perked up at hearing about my scribelike effort with Proverbs. Rachel told us she'd just gotten a new Bible with lots of blank space on the sides of each page so she could journal in the margins. Seanique said she was planning to get a Bible just like that. And Kathryn was doing a study in the books of Psalms and Proverbs. The more we chatted, the more we realized we shared a common faith.

When you talk with people about things that are more significant than the weather—the things that matter to you, like your family and your faith—it doesn't just foster good communication; it begins to form a bond of trust. I remember thinking, *This is a group I'd like to have dinner with.*

* * *

The five of us welcomed 144 passengers to the next leg of our flight from LaGuardia to Dallas, bringing the total on board to 149. One was a Southwest employee, William, who was on his way to Texas for leadership training. He gave his cabin seat to a customer and took an open flight-attendant jump seat at the back of the plane.

After grabbing a couple of cans of water from the galley, I settled into my seat in the cockpit. At 10:27 a.m. Darren and I pushed back from the gate and started the engines. Sometimes LaGuardia traffic is so busy that you can get stuck in a slow-moving "conga line" waiting for your turn to depart. But that day our time from gate to takeoff was quick—one of the easiest turnarounds at LaGuardia I'd ever done. I taxied, and Darren had the radios. But it was Darren's turn to fly, so when we received takeoff clearance from Tower, we switched. He took the aircraft, and I covered the radios.

The day looked pretty clear. There would be no significant weather to dodge between New York and Dallas. Our scheduled flight time was three hours and forty-seven minutes, but winds were favorable, and it looked like we would be able to shave off about twenty of those minutes.

As Darren flew, I talked with air traffic control, switching frequencies from Tower to Departure, then began the higher-altitude frequency changes with New York Center. As always, when we reached ten thousand feet, I rang the flight attendants. Climbing through eighteen thousand feet, Darren and I changed the altimeter setting to "two-niner-niner-two." Everything was routine.

New York Center cleared us to climb to our cruising altitude at thirty-eight thousand feet. Passing through twenty-eight thousand feet, we received a traffic call from our controller saying that another aircraft was heading toward us from left to right a few miles away. I narrowed the scale on my flight display to find the traffic on TCAS (Traffic Collision Avoidance System). The other plane was not a factor. Traveling at five hundred miles per hour, we continued to climb, now somewhere over eastern Pennsylvania, headed west-southwest toward Texas.

We had been airborne for about twenty minutes and were

passing 32,500 feet when it felt like a Mack truck hit my side of the aircraft. My first thought was that we *had* been hit—that we'd had a midair collision. Darren and I both grabbed the controls and watched as the left engine instruments flashed and wound down.

A moment later, truly the tiniest slice of a second later, we couldn't see *anything*. The jump seat oxygen masks and fire gloves went flying from their storage compartments and bounced around in the cockpit with other loose items. The aircraft began to shudder so violently that we couldn't focus our eyes. The cockpit filled with a cloud of smoke, which made me think there was a fire, but the fire alarm wasn't ringing. It was like being inside a snow globe that someone was shaking, hard.

Just as suddenly, a deafening roar enveloped us. We couldn't see, we couldn't breathe, and a piercing pain stabbed our ears, all while the aircraft snapped into a rapid roll and skidded hard to the left as the nose of the aircraft pitched over, initiating a dive toward the ground.

★   ★   ★

It's a luxury of storytelling that I can pause here to explain what had happened, though none of us aboard Flight 1380 knew any of these details at the time.

The initial sensation of being hit by a truck was brought on when a piece of a turbine fan blade in the left engine broke off and caused catastrophic engine damage. The explosion caused the leading edge of the engine cowling to disintegrate—I heard pieces of it were found scattered across the Pennsylvania countryside— and the rest of the cowling around the engine to roll back like a banana peel. It remained attached at the aft end of the engine, flailing around in the wind. What was once sleek and aerodynamic was now more like a barn door swinging in a hurricane. Shrapnel from the explosion took chunks out of the leading edge of the wing and the tail, ripped a panel open underneath the wing, and severed hydraulic lines around the engine. A fuel line was also cut above the cut-off valve, so we had no way of shutting off the fuel that was flowing out of the left fuel tank.

A piece of debris hit the window at row 14, causing it to fail and blow out, which is what generated the deafening roar and the sudden loss of pressure in the cockpit and the cabin. If you've ever been in a car when someone rolls down the window at sixty miles an hour, the noise is unpleasant. I don't have words to adequately describe the ear-drum punishment of a five-hundred-mile-per-hour experience.

When the airplane's window broke, it was like a pinprick to an inflated balloon. All of the air rushed out of the aircraft to equalize the pressure with the outside air. The sudden pressure differential caused the piercing pain in our ears that ran down our necks. While this wasn't debilitating, it certainly added to the intensity of the moment.

Though we practice the emergency procedures for rapid depressurization in the flight simulator, we don't practice the physiological effects. Just as air was pulled out of the aircraft, it was pulled out of our lungs. Until we could get our oxygen masks on, we were left gasping for our next breath.

The combined damage on the left side of the aircraft is what caused the violent shuddering, because instead of an engine under the left wing, we now had what amounted to an anchor. The huge asymmetry (the difference between a dead and severely damaged engine on the left and a healthy engine on the right producing thrust) immediately pushed the nose of the aircraft hard to the left. That rotation caused the outside wing to generate more lift than the wing on the inside of the turn, which made the aircraft roll rapidly toward the bad engine.

Flight, even in turbulence, has a feeling of air around the aircraft. This event felt like we were flying through a canyon of boulders, hitting most of them as we went. We tried shouting at each other but couldn't hear a word, so we resorted to hand signals. At our altitude, and with a punctured cabin, we had about sixty seconds to make some important decisions before we became oxygen deprived. Working together, we stopped the roll at a little over 40 degrees angle of bank and stomped on the right rudder to pull the nose around. It was Darren's leg of the trip, so with a head nod and a show of my hands off the controls, I let him know he was still flying. I had released the controls to him.

He got his mask on first, and as I put on my mask, I recalled my days as an out-of-control flight instructor. *This has a familiar feel . . . not welcome, but familiar*, I thought. The Boeing 737 (all the models that I'm familiar with, from the old 200 through the newest Max 8) are incredibly well-built aircraft; however, they aren't designed for sudden changes to the aircraft's trajectory, especially at high altitudes and with a heavy load. But the explosion had caused exactly that. The immediate loss of thrust on one side and drag created on the other, along with the skid and roll, caused the nose of the aircraft to pitch over and initiate a descent.

The aircraft would not have stayed at altitude had we tried to keep it there. We had to work *with* the plane, not against it, because in the thin air of high altitudes, 737s are not designed to be "yanked and banked" like a Hornet. The combination of high altitude and heavy weight requires a steady hand, a very judicious one, because the margin for error is reduced. Translating this into aviator lingo, that means an aircraft becomes "squirrelly" in such conditions. Flying in it is a little like driving on black ice. You can do it but only if you steer gently.

The plane wanted to descend, so we let it. Some of the passengers later described it as being "in a free fall." I can understand how it felt like that. Later, flight data showed that in the first minute after the explosion, the aircraft lost 2,700 feet. In the second minute, we descended another 4,300 feet. In the third, 3,500. In the fourth, 4,500. And in the fifth, 3,400. These were all large increments of descent, totaling more than 18,000 feet lost in the first five minutes alone. While that was certainly faster than a normal descent of about 2,500 feet per minute, it was not out of control.

In those first few minutes—when we were descending rapidly, trying to maintain control of the aircraft, and not fully aware of what we were up against—we had a laundry list of things to do. First, we needed to slow down to see if we could reduce the shuddering and shaking. I wasn't sure how much more battering the aircraft could take before something else failed and we had a worse situation to deal with. We obviously needed the big pieces to remain attached in order to land. And to land, we needed to be able to focus our eyes on and read our instruments and checklists.

The age-old aviation maxim "aviate, navigate, communicate" immediately came to mind. We were in control of the aircraft, so we had aviate under control, at least for the moment. Now we needed to navigate toward a place to land. After departing LaGuardia, we had essentially flown west-southwest on our way to Texas. The explosion and subsequent push of the right engine's thrust had us pointing south as we descended.

Where should we land? It was time to communicate.

★ ★ ★

"SWA1380, if you're trying to get to me, all I hear is static."

When I first contacted air traffic control, I thought we had a fire, possibly in the engine. Where else would the smoke have come from? I repeated the information: "SWA1380 has an engine fire, descending."

"SWA1380, you're descending right now?"

"Yes, sir," I said. "We're single engine. Descending. Have a fire. Number one."

"All right, SWA1380," the controller said. "Where would you like to go to? Which airport?"

"Give us a vector for your closest," I said.

Darren pointed out Philadelphia on his map, which was scaled out farther than mine. It was a great option, with long runways and first responders at the field. Besides that, it was a familiar airport to both of us, and I liked the idea of something familiar. I quickly added, "Philadelphia."

ATC gave us a vector for Philly.

The controller asked for clarification: "SWA1380, so you're single engine, cause of fire?"

At this point I realized there was no longer any indication of a fire anywhere on the aircraft, inside or out. I revised my information. "Actually, no fire now. But we are single engine."

"Okay. You are single engine, cleared to Philly. Can you maintain eleven thousand [feet]?"

"Yes, sir," I said.

He gave the clearance. "SWA1380, descend and maintain eleven thousand."

"Okay, down to eleven thousand," I said. "If you would . . . have them roll the trucks. It's engine number one. The captain's side."

Throughout the descent, whenever we made a left turn

toward Philadelphia, the aircraft wanted to roll over on the left side. Darren and I refused to let the plane get too much angle of bank during these turns. Had we allowed that, the risk of flipping over would have been high and our chance of recovering would have been slim. Darren did a great job of keeping control of the aircraft.

With the situation somewhat in hand and knowing that I had a plane full of people in fear for their lives, I turned my attention to the cabin. There weren't just 144 passengers and three flight attendants behind the cockpit door. Everyone back there had a name—beginning with the three I knew: Rachel, Seanique, and Kathryn. Only a few minutes had passed since the explosion, but a few minutes can seem like an eternity to someone in a life-threatening situation.

Before I pushed the flight attendant call button, I made a cabin announcement but doubted anyone would be able to hear it. The deafening roar still drowned out every other sound. Fortunately, and I would say providentially, many people *did* hear me—including the flight attendants, who couldn't hear me over the interphone. They could make out my simple message, a message of hope:

"We are not going down," I said. "We are going to Philly."

CHAPTER 14

CRISIS IN THE CABIN

Do all the good you can, by all the means you can, in all the ways you can.

—JOHN WESLEY

As chaotic as things were in the cockpit, they were worse in the cabin. Even as we regained control, the plane continued its bone-jarring shudder. Passengers screamed, cried, prayed, held hands, and sent messages to loved ones on the ground. Oxygen masks were dangling from the overhead compartments, but only a few people had them on correctly. In the confusion, some panicked passengers rejected Kathryn's attempts to help.

Seanique, Rachel, and Kathryn strapped on their portable oxygen bottles, put on the masks, and unbuckled from their jump seats. Then they began the dangerous process of moving through the cabin, helping people secure their oxygen masks and assuring them that we had a destination—we were going to Philadelphia.

It's important to me that you know the extreme risks these women took in that setting to unbuckle and get out of their seats. Some might think they were simply doing their job; they did more than their job that day. They would have been justified to stay seated, as they were placing their own lives at risk to do otherwise. Setting aside concerns for their own well-being, all three women *chose* to get up. With the rapid depressurization, they knew there was a hole in the aircraft somewhere (they didn't know where at first), and it was possible that at any moment some other part of the aircraft might tear away and take them with it.

As they stumbled down the aisle, they took a beating. They were struck by flying debris. They sustained strained backs and bruised ribs from bouncing off the seats, and the oxygen bottle straps lacerated their necks. Everyone on board had been affected by the rapid depressurization just as Darren and I had been, with shooting pain in their ears and the terrifying feeling of not being able to breathe. But one by one, shouting over the din while they also paused to help people, the attendants went from seat to seat, yelling, "We're going to be okay! We're going to Philly!"

Afterward the passengers shared how that one simple message made all the difference. It changed the attitude inside the aircraft. They were still worried, and they continued to pray and send messages to loved ones, but the panic began to subside. A sense of calm had room to move in and supplant the blinding fear that accompanies thoughts of all the terrible things that might happen. And though the words didn't change the circumstances, terror was replaced with possibility.

We were still in a crippled aircraft hurtling through the sky, but now both passengers and crew knew Darren and I had control of the aircraft and were endeavoring to get it safely on the ground. We all had something to wrap our minds around: a destination. And with that destination came hope, which changed all of us.

In row 8 was a mother of a six-month-old baby who kept trying to take off her oxygen mask. Andrew Needum, sitting ahead of her in row 7, noticed the mother's struggle to keep it on. Andrew, on the flight with his parents, his wife, and their two children, was a firefighter and emergency medical technician from Celina, Texas. After making sure his family was secure and had oxygen, Andrew exchanged a knowing look with his wife. The situation was dire, but helping people was what he did.

With his wife's understanding, Andrew unbuckled and turned around to help the mother. Getting the baby's mask secure took a couple of tries because the elastic strap had come loose from its coupling and had to be reattached. As he worked on it, he noticed a commotion several rows behind him.

*   *   *

Rachel was the first flight attendant to arrive at the scene in row 14, where shrapnel from the engine explosion had broken and blown out the window. As it did, the force had pulled the window-seat passenger toward the window. Still secured by her seatbelt, which anchored her inside, her upper body had been pulled outside.

Hollie Mackey, a professor from Oklahoma, had moved from her aisle seat to the middle seat to grab the woman's belt loops, attempting to pull her back in, but she wasn't strong enough. The suction was too great. The young passenger Mackey switched seats with was buckled in the aisle seat, so Rachel immediately crouched in the floor space in front of them and grabbed onto the woman's thighs, joining the effort to bring her back in.

In row 15, Tim McGinty, a cattle rancher and Realtor from Hillsboro, Texas, tore off his oxygen mask and seatbelt and leaned across the seatbacks to help Hollie and Rachel pull the injured passenger back inside. That's when Andrew joined the effort. He laid himself across the laps of the passengers in the aisle and center seats. As someone in the aisle grabbed his ankles, Andrew put all of his weight into pulling the woman back in, but he had no leverage.

It seemed like a hopeless situation. Andrew slid back into the aisle, stood up, and yelled to Hollie and the young lady, "I'm sorry, but you're going to have to move!"

Rachel took the two female passengers up the turbulent aisle to her and Seanique's jump seats in the front of the aircraft. She strapped them in while Andrew and Tim tried again. With more space in the row, Andrew positioned himself in front of the woman, with Tim once again leaning over the seat. Both men pulled, but the force working against them was still incredibly strong. Andrew slid his arm out through the window in an attempt to grab the passenger's shoulder. The air outside was paralyzingly cold, and the force of the wind instantly pinned his arm. The men weren't making any progress, but they were determined not to give up.

* * *

In an emergency situation it's the captain's responsibility to land the plane, regardless of whose turn it is to fly, so I took over the controls. My first impression was that they felt sluggish and unresponsive, a little "gritty," as if we were flying through gravel.

The intercom dinged with a call from Seanique. She had terrible news. She told us that a window had broken and a passenger had been pulled through the opening. Other passengers were attempting to get her back inside but had not yet been able to do so. We had slowed to about three hundred miles per hour, but they needed us to slow down even more.

Darren and I looked at each other. For the first time we understood what had caused the rapid depressurization.

In the cabin Andrew and Tim said they could feel the deceleration. The lower speed reduced the force of the air rushing past the window, which allowed them to finally be able to pull the woman back inside. Andrew could see she was unconscious and bleeding and most likely had sustained fatal injuries. Yet there was always a chance. He unbuckled her seatbelt and laid her across the row of seats. Then he felt for a pulse as Seanique put out a call for anyone who knew CPR.

A retired school nurse named Peggy Phillips was on board. After the explosion she had sent a single text to her daughter: "Plane trouble. I love you." Peggy knew CPR and had also been trained in crisis management. When the call came for help, she immediately stood up and made herself known to Rachel. Peggy and Andrew performed CPR while Rachel retrieved the emergency medical kit.

Back in the cockpit I had my hands full maintaining control of the aircraft and communicating with air traffic control while Darren ran checklists, helped me with radio frequency changes, managed the damaged systems, and kept in touch with the flight attendants. Our reduced speed minimized the aircraft's shudder and allowed us to focus on our instruments a little better. The noise diminished slightly too. As we descended below ten thousand feet, we were able to take off our masks, but we still had trouble hearing the flight attendants over the intercom.

Darren and I had a number of emergency-procedure checklists that we were trying to run. There was the rapid-depressurization checklist, the engine severe-damage checklist, and the emergency-descent checklist. We were leaking fuel as well as hydraulic fluid and had lost our hydraulic A system engine-driven pump.

Each of these situations was an emergency in itself and had associated checklists. We needed to do the single-engine descent checklist, the single-engine approach checklist, and finally, when configured for landing, the single-engine-before-landing checklist.

All of these emergency checklists are meant to be run with both pilots involved. Darren would read the challenge and the response, I would echo that response and verify the relevant switch or gauge reading, and he would carry out the required task. As we descended toward Philadelphia, however, Darren couldn't get a word into the confusion. ATC had a lot of questions and put us through numerous frequency changes. He was also trying to be available to Kathryn, Seanique, and Rachel with real-time information and answers to their questions.

"Southwest 1380, descend and maintain six thousand," the controller instructed me.

"Southwest 1380, down to six thousand," I said.

"And when you get a chance," he said, "I need fuel remaining and souls-on-board."

"One hundred and forty-nine souls on board," I said. "Five-plus hours of fuel."

"Can I get the fuel in pounds and the exact nature of the emergency, please?" the controller asked.

"Engine has severe damage. Engine failure. And exact pounds of fuel . . ." I paused to add it up while my mic was still keyed. Pounds of fuel wasn't a typical emergency request, and honestly, I was a bit busy to have to stop and add it up. But I assumed ATC had their reasons for needing the information in a new format.

"Twenty-one thousand pounds," I eventually said. In spite of our severed fuel lines, we would be landing nearly ten thousand pounds overweight, still carrying most of the fuel we should have burned on the way to Dallas.

"SWA1380, you gonna go right in, or do you need extended final?"

"Extended final," I said. Darren had requested more time in order to get all those checklists done.

We were cleared to four thousand feet, then heard a considerable amount of chatter as the controller moved other aircraft out of the way so we could get in to Philadelphia first. When that was settled, they gave us the approach frequency and asked us to maintain four thousand feet. We tried to level off, but it took us a little longer than we had anticipated to stabilize our descent.

The controller asked: "Do you need further assistance? What type of final do you want? I heard—short, or long?"

"Yes," I said. "We're going to need a long final."

"Okay," the controller said. "SWA1380, you'll be landing 27 left. Just let me know when you need to turn base. Right now, I only have one plane in front of you, which is a Southwest. I'm sure he'll pull right off if you need to go in." We heard more chatter as he cleared more airplanes out of the way; then we were cleared once again to another frequency.

Philadelphia Approach came on and said, "I understand you're in an emergency. Let me know when you want to go in."

"We have part of the aircraft missing," I said. "We're gonna need to slow down a bit."

"SWA1380, speed is your discretion," he said. "Maintain your altitude above three thousand. You let me know when you want to turn base."

"All right," I said. "Down to three thousand; 210 [knots] on the speed."

"Absolutely," Approach said. "You let me know anything you need." We heard more chatter as he kept the area clear.

"SWA1380 wants the turn now," I said.

"SWA1380, start turning southbound," he said. "There's a SWA737 on a four-mile final, will be turning southbound. Start looking for the airport. It's off to your right and slightly behind you there. Altitude is your discretion. Use caution for the downtown area. Advise you to maintain at or above twenty-two hundred."

"Okay, can you have medical meet us on the runway? We've got injured passengers."

"Injured passengers, okay. And is your airplane physically on fire?"

"No, it's not on fire," I said. "But part of it is missing. They said there's a hole and, uh"—I wasn't exactly sure how to relay this information—"someone went out."

Approach seemed caught off guard by this news. After a brief pause he said, "I'm sorry. You said there was a hole and somebody went out?"

Darren and I looked at each other and shook our heads; it was too complicated for a radio call. I couldn't form a reply. There was nothing more to add, and I couldn't allow myself to get sidetracked by the thought of that dire situation in the cabin. I had to fly the airplane.

"Southwest 1380, we'll work it out," he said. "The airport is just off to your right. Report it in sight, please."

A few seconds later I saw it. "In sight," I said.

"You're cleared visual approach, 27 left," he said, then handed us off to Tower.

Darren set up the flight management computer on board to show us the airspeed for a single-engine, Flaps 15 landing, which would have been suitable for a simple engine-failure scenario. But now I could see more clearly out my side window the severe damage to our left wing, as well as feel the drag on the controls and entire aircraft as we slowed our descent. I told Darren I wanted Flaps 5 instead.

This isn't a typical position used for landings, but with that damage I didn't want to move anything on the wing that I didn't have to. Also, with our plane so heavy with the extra fuel, I was concerned that we might not be able to make the runway with the added drag that would be generated by using Flaps 15. Flaps allow the aircraft to fly a slower airspeed for landing, but like everything in life, there is a trade-off, and I didn't need that particular trade. More airspeed gave me more rudder authority, and I couldn't afford more drag.

Darren didn't even hesitate. "What speed do you want?" he asked me. He had no time to get buried deep in "the box" (the flight management computer) to dig up that information.

I said, "One eighty," which was a ballpark Flaps 5 landing-pattern speed, and it would put us below the maximum tire speed at touchdown.

At this point we had passed north of the field and turned to the south in our final descent to get to Philadelphia. Darren needed a longer final approach to finish preparing the aircraft for landing, but I was having an uneasy feeling about that. As we drew closer to Philadelphia and I was mulling it over, our only option became very clear.

When I tried to level off, I realized I couldn't add enough thrust to maintain airspeed *and* altitude. The amount of rudder it took to keep the aircraft in balanced flight now became the limiting factor in how much power I could add from the right engine. If I added too much, I wouldn't have enough rudder authority to overcome the asymmetric thrust, and it would push the nose to the left, causing even more drag. So there was a point at which adding power became detrimental, which meant I had another trade-off to consider. If I wanted to stop descending, I would have to give up airspeed. If I wanted to keep my airspeed, I would have to sacrifice altitude. It became clear that if I didn't manage this well, it might not end well.

Darren had been trying to get an update from the flight attendants on the situation in the cabin but couldn't get a response. Growing concerned, he started to unbuckle to look back and check on them, but at that moment Seanique called to say the medical situation was dire. We needed to get on the ground quickly.

The time for checklists was over. Darren told her that we would be on the ground soon and to prepare the cabin for landing. We had to turn toward the airport now and would just have to focus on getting the checklist items that were absolutely required for a safe landing done within the limited time we had available. We signed off with Approach, and Darren switched to Tower frequency. The tower controller told us we were cleared to land.

It is not uncommon to shoot approaches with the autopilot engaged, but I would continue to hand fly this one. The explosion had kicked the autopilot off, and, frankly, the thought never crossed my mind to reengage it. Darren and I hand flew the aircraft throughout the entire descent.

I had Darren select Visual Flight Path on my HGS (Heads-up Guidance System) so I would have a 3-degree glide path reference for my approach to the runway. Because we don't typically land Flaps 5, even when practicing single-engine approaches, the sight picture as I looked at the runway would be very different from what I was accustomed. With the lower flap setting, the nose of the aircraft would be higher than normal, but the symbology in the HGS combiner glass would be familiar. We also would be flying about 50 knots (almost 60 miles an hour) faster than normal, which would also change the sight picture. But since I use the HGS for every approach, I wanted a little slice of normal for this anything-but-normal approach.

With the decision made to head directly for the airport rather than take extra time to work through more checklists, I had one more 90-degree right turn to go to line up with the runway. That is when things took a turn for the worse. I had already made a 90-degree right turn when I was over the city and heading east, but I had done that while still descending and with the right engine at idle power. Now, heading south, I had added power to slow our descent. When I put in the controls to make the final right turn that would line us up with the runway, absolutely nothing happened.

There was a brief moment of silence on the radio as well as in the cockpit. Months later, when Darren and I had the opportunity to listen to the cockpit voice recording of that flight, we heard the silence broken with two words from me that formed a question.

"Heavenly Father?"

While I certainly remember thinking it, I didn't realize I had said it out loud. Darren didn't hear me at all. He was looking out his window, watching the airport starting to pass by on the right, and wondering when I was going to turn.

For a brief moment I continued that conversation with my heavenly Father.

Lord, what am I missing?

There was nothing I could do about the weight of the aircraft or the extreme drag hanging off the left wing. My only option was in the palm of my right hand. The answer was clear, but it was not what I wanted. I was already concerned about the energy state and my ability to even make it to the runway, so the last thing I wanted to do was pull power on my good engine and sacrifice airspeed *and* altitude. But it was clear that I didn't have a choice. The aircraft simply would not turn right with all of the drag pulling the left wing backward and all of the thrust from the good engine pushing the right wing forward.

I made the decision. I eased the right throttle back, stood on the right rudder, and fed in some ailerons (input that tells the aircraft which way to turn). And it worked! As the nose slowly swung around to the right, and we were finally headed toward a nice long piece of concrete, I called for landing gear down. We were getting close, but we weren't there yet.

* * *

I knew I had one shot at landing. There was only so much power I could add before it overcame my rudder authority to keep the plane pointing at the runway, and that power setting, now with the added drag of my landing gear, had us decelerating and in a descent. There would be no second chance this time, no missed approach, and no go-around.

We did the before-landing checklist, assuring that the gear, flaps, and speedbrakes were configured for landing. Darren confirmed that the flap inhibit switch was up. This would keep us from receiving a warning that our flaps weren't in a normal position for landing. He asked me if I wanted autobrakes, which would have been standard in a single-engine landing situation, but I decided not to use them. We had a long runway in front of us, and our passengers had already endured a horribly rough ride. I wanted to at least give them a smooth landing and rollout.

I could also see that the fire trucks were at the far end of the runway, so I intended to let the aircraft roll down to them. I wasn't sure about the nature of the injuries our passengers had sustained, but I did know we needed to get medical help on the aircraft as quickly as possible.

The plane slowed as we descended toward the runway. At seven hundred feet we were doing 170 knots, or 194 miles per hour. We touched down at 165 knots, or about 30 knots faster than normal, but 15 knots slower than my target. The usual margin for error in approach speed is only 5 knots below the target airspeed. However, had I held my speed, we would not have made the runway.

In the cabin, Andrew and Peggy were still doing CPR when the flight attendants began instructing passengers to get in the position for an emergency landing. We had not instructed them to do this, but as they saw the ground whipping by the windows about 50 miles per hour faster than normal, they didn't take any chances. Their forward thinking is one of the things I love about those ladies.

"Heads down! Stay down! Brace! Brace! Brace!"

Andrew told Peggy to get down, and she did. He kept doing chest compressions on the injured woman. He saw the flight attendants standing or sitting in the aisle without seatbelts, having given up their jump seats to displaced passengers.

At 11:23 a.m. we were on the ground.

"Nice Air Force landing," Darren said.

As we rolled out, the cockpit voice recorder captured me saying, "Thank You, Lord. Thank You, thank You, Lord." That was a prayer I do remember saying out loud.

CHAPTER 15

RELIEF AND GRIEF

There is a time for everything,
and a season for every activity under the
heavens . . .
a time to weep and a time to laugh,
a time to mourn and a time to dance.

—ECCLESIASTES 3:1–4 NIV

We touched down in Philadelphia twenty minutes after the explosion. With our wheels on the ground, I felt a sense of relief. Yet I knew there was still a terrible situation in the cabin.

We taxied quickly to the end of the runway, then off to where a circle of fire trucks and paramedics waited nearby. Fuel and hydraulic fluid continued to leak out after we landed, and firefighters sprayed down the area.

People react in a variety of ways when a plane makes an emergency landing. When they feel the ground underneath them and know the plane is no longer moving, they sometimes rush to get out as quickly as they can. But it's a ten- to twelve-foot drop from an open 737 door to the ground, and broken bones or sprains can result even when slides are used.

After we landed, I put the flaps to 40 degrees in case anyone opened the over-wing doors and tried to rush out of the aircraft. At that angle the flaps would create a little bit of a slide to the ground, reducing the drop and the potential for injury. I called back to the flight attendants and asked if they saw any smoke or fire outside. I also told them to put the "girt bars up" to prevent the slides from deploying when the aircraft doors were opened. I wanted passengers to use airstairs instead, which ground crews needed to bring to the plane. It would be a few minutes before the stairs got there, and with six exit doors and only three flight attendants, passengers could have gone out a door if they wanted to.

I shut down the right engine, and Darren and I went over the shutdown checklist. As soon as we were done, I left the aircraft in Darren's capable hands and headed back to check on the flight attendants and passengers.

When I unlocked the cockpit door and stepped through, I could not have been more surprised. Instead of finding a group of frightened, anxious, and angry passengers, I was met with composed, attentive people.

At this point there were a few people in the forward galley area. Rachel and Seanique were there with debris stuck in their windblown hair; Kathryn was in the rear section of the aircraft. Others, who I would learn later included Andrew and Tim, some paramedics, and the FBI, were also there. It was a bit crowded.

Someone said, "Where did you come from?" My hair was not windblown like the flight attendants', and no one had seen me offering any help during the flight.

Someone else said, "I'd like to shake the hand of the guy who landed this bird!"

I can't help but be flattered when I'm mistaken for a flight attendant, especially as I get older.

"I landed this bird," I said good-naturedly as I reached for the PA to speak to the passengers.

"Thank you for your patience," I said to them. "I am sorry. I know this was a rough ride. God is good, and we are on the ground. Thank you for staying seated while we take care of our medical emergency first. There are stairs on the way, and if you want to gather your things—" As soon as I said that, passengers started to stand up. Who could blame them? I quickly added, "Please just gather the things where you're seated; we'll have the airstairs here soon." To my amazement everybody immediately returned to their seats.

Paramedics, firefighters, FBI agents, and mechanics had climbed an extension ladder to board the plane. The paramedics quickly took charge of our injured passenger and used a sturdy transporter called a MegaMover to deliver her to the medical team on the ground. The FBI agents were there to determine if the explosion was an act of terrorism. They concluded that it was not.

Because we couldn't predict when the airstairs would arrive, I asked the flight attendants to start a water service to the passengers, but by the time I asked I realized they'd already served a third of the cabin, needing no prompting from me. All three women could barely speak. Their throats were raw from shouting, but there they were, still continuing to serve. They will always be among the first people who come to mind when I think of sacrificial, compassionate service.

I started to move through the cabin, taking time to speak to and look into each person's eyes, quietly grateful that they would soon be returning to their lives and loved ones. I usually walk down the aisle of the aircraft if we have a lengthy delay or have had something out of the ordinary happen. We all handle life better when the mysteries are minimized and our questions get answers. The proverbial buck stops with the captain of the aircraft, so I make it a point to make myself available to my passengers to answer their questions whenever I can.

Walking through, I remember a few moments in particular. I recall the baby girl, Sophie, now sleeping soundly on her mother's lap, precious and at peace, trusting her mother in slumber. I stopped to inquire about her, and her mom calmly replied she was fine. I remember the brave face of Andrew's young daughter. We spoke about the doll she was holding, who was also "fine."

I continued through the plane, asking each person if he or she was okay, listening as best I could, and answering questions to the best of my ability. Throughout this time a part of my mind was always on the passenger who *wasn't* okay. I believe there was a terrible clarity in all our minds about the tragedy that had occurred.

All was quiet as I returned back up the aisle.

When the airstairs arrived, I helped people with their bags and gave each of them a hug or a high five as they exited. I didn't really have to think about these gestures. How would I want my parents or my children to be treated after such a traumatic event? That wasn't a hard question to answer either. In return I received nothing but expressions of politeness, courtesy, gratitude, and relief. This unfiltered generosity of spirit spoke to me about who these passengers were every day, not just at that moment.

*   *   *

When all the passengers were safely off the plane, I took a moment to glance around the cabin. With all of the oxygen masks still down, I closed my eyes briefly and offered a prayer of thanks. So many things had gone wrong that day, but so many things had gone right too. The distance between the explosion and Philadelphia was just the right distance for us to have made it to Philly. We couldn't have made an airport any farther away. My inclination to use Flaps 5 had turned out to be the right choice. Everything had gone as well as it possibly could have in the circumstances, right down to the moment when we lowered our gear and turned in. Nothing was perfect, but everything worked.

I went back into the cockpit and started pulling my things together. I packed up my headset and flight bag, stowed my oxygen mask, and put the HGS in the retracted position. Darren had taken care of everything else. I collected my bags and set them aside, then pulled out my phone to text my family.

I snapped a picture of the left engine with its shredded cowling and sent it to Dean with this line of text: Single engine landing in Philly.

Your aircraft? he texted back.

I wouldn't claim it as mine, I wrote. But I did fly it.

Everyone in my family responded as I would have guessed. When I texted Sydney, she said, Mom, I love you. I'm so glad you're okay.

Then I texted Marshall, who quipped, There's a reason

Southwest gives you two. He was in class at the time, "transmitting in the blind"—aviation slang for not having any idea what is going on. He thought I had taken a bird in the engine and turned around to land. "No big deal," he would say later. I thought it would have been a big deal either way.

I sent a quick text to Mom and Dad. They would tell my siblings.

I received a text from a dear friend, Linda Maloney: Hey girl . . . news travels fast . . . praying for u.

Linda, an aviator from the Navy, had once had to eject from an A-6. She knew to save her words until later. I love her!

Thx, God is good, I replied.

Darren and I walked out of Flight 1380 together and down the stairs into the waiting medical van. He went with one EMT while I went with another. As per standard procedure, I had my blood drawn. They took my pulse and did an EKG. The EMT looked up at me.

"How do you get through security with those nerves of steel?"

"Pardon me?" I said, pulling my wandering thoughts back to the gentleman in front of me.

"You don't even have an elevated heart rate!" he said. "You're completely calm." He checked my stats again.

Although I'd like to take credit for such nerves of steel, I'm as human as the next person. I believe my calm voice and pulse rate that day were the product of more than my training and demeanor. They didn't magically appear in a sudden moment of need. They'd developed over the years, nurtured through each life experience by my faith and confidence in God's goodness.

As with aircraft, it's the Designer that I am truly in awe of. I admire the Maker of the "nerves of steel" that showed up in so many people during that forty-minute flight.

★ ★ ★

The survival of many can never eclipse the loss of one. My crew and I felt the value of human life that day. Though we returned 148 people to their lives and loved ones, we were not able to do that for Jennifer Riordan. The loss of this young wife, mother, bank executive, and philanthropist who was seated in 14A will always weigh heavy on my heart, my crew's hearts, and my company's heart.

It is true that if we can find words to express the turmoil within ourselves, we can sort it out and eventually get through it. Right after the ordeal Dean sensed the turmoil in me—even over the phone. For three decades my husband has been my best friend and favorite pilot, and his presence in my life has given me an almost unfair advantage. He has flown the same aircraft I have in the same career I have. He understands everything about my job and can almost see the world I live in from behind my own eyes. Dean is a big reason that I have been able to keep life, including the influence of Flight 1380, in perspective.

As the dust settled and I found my heart in conflict with itself, Dean reminded me that it's possible to grieve and rejoice at the same time. He pointed me to a beautiful scriptural poem we both love:

> There is . . .
>> a time to weep and a time to laugh,
>> a time to mourn and a time to dance.
> (Ecclesiastes 3:1, 4 NIV)

April 17, 2018 was the day I fully understood those words.

CHAPTER 16

HABITS, HOPE, AND HEROES

"Do as I did."

—JESUS, AS HE WASHED ANOTHER'S FEET (JOHN 13:15)

When I was a kid, if a horse, hog, or steer got the best of me, threw me off, or pushed past me, Dad would give me a knowing nod that meant "Go get 'em." No matter how upset I was, I had to retrieve the offender and get back in the saddle or put the outlaw back in its proper pen. I grew up thinking the reason for that was to teach the animal a lesson: crime doesn't pay.

It turned out the lesson wasn't for them at all.

The lesson was for me.

Things in life will often throw us down, slip out of our grasp, or push us aside to get past us. How do we handle these experiences? "Go get 'em" echoes in my mind.

On a regular basis throughout my life, I've reevaluated my purpose and goals and adjusted my approach. Motive and merit are the guide rails that help me keep my focus and my nerve.

It's always easier to see the value of the turbulence in life after we've gone through it. In my life, both on the ground and in the air, all the things that went wrong gave me a chance to work through problems and make decisions, drawing from what I had taken the time to study, learn, or memorize. While I don't like the interruptions that problems present—I don't enjoy learning lessons any more than the next person—those times seasoned me, groomed and prepared me.

The lessons I learned from the seasons of turbulence in my life are what I drew on when I needed to fly and land Flight 1380.

*   *   *

Southwest was generous with the flight and cabin crew. They gave us more time off than we asked for, with the option to fly anytime we wanted to during that hiatus. I went back to work in May, three and a half weeks after the incident, for a number of reasons.

First, because I wanted to. I continue to love flying, and I enjoy my job. Flying is a much-needed slice of normal in my life. I also thought it was important for my family, and anyone else who was watching, to see I still had confidence in flight, in Southwest Airlines, and in Boeing aircraft. And last, I didn't want any falsehoods about the incident to take root, whether in my mind or anyone else's.

Flight 1380 was not a typical flight, and aviation is still one of the safest modes of transportation we have. Few people stop driving after having been in or seen a car accident. Though each person will have his or her own unique timing, I think we all can choose to be resilient. We can choose to get back up, to press on with the gift of life, to live without fear. This is what I chose.

When I think about that day, that flight, it's not the machinery that comes to mind, not the exploded engine or the aircraft that didn't want to fly, and not the myriad decisions Darren and I had to make. I find myself thinking about the people. The selfless actions, the unprompted sacrifice, and the compassion shown by the flight attendants. By Andrew, Tim, and Peggy. And by so many of the passengers on board.

After difficult experiences we each get up and dust ourselves off at different paces and in different ways. I had a few more years of flying experience than my crew members and, most likely, more hours in an aircraft than any of my passengers. My history helped to give me a seasoned perspective and perhaps a few more tools in my toolkit, so to speak, to help me move past the incident.

I was not fearful of returning to the cockpit. I believed the words I had often read, then passed on to my son and daughter during those adolescent years: "God has not given us a spirit of timidity (fear), but of power, love, and self-control" (2 Timothy 1:7, paraphrased). Words have meaning, and depending on where they come from, they also have weight.

*   *   *

I'm writing these words almost a year to the day after Flight 1380 landed in Philadelphia. Since then I've tried to put my experience into words, for my own sake and so I can share my takeaways from such an experience. I've had the chance to meet some of my passengers, either through correspondence or at gatherings such as a Christmas parade. They have been universally wonderful and are still working through some of the things that happened that day, as I am. As I think about it today, my takeaway from Flight 1380 is threefold.

First, habits—good and bad—become instincts under pressure. In other words, the choices we make every day become our reflex on bad days.

Animals have instincts, many of which serve them well, but how they react to things isn't really a matter of conscious choice. If you've ever seen a deer run into a fence or dash across a busy highway, you know what I'm talking about. The element of reason is missing.

Humans are built differently. We've been given the gift of choice—choice in how we behave and what we believe, for example. Our habits, the things we do so routinely that we don't even think about them much, are an extraordinary expression of choice—to choose to drink tea or coffee in the morning, to save or spend money, to exercise or rest, to play or work overtime. Our habits arise out of what we believe and what we choose.

One of my habits is to put my day before the Lord when I wake up. I realize there are numerous belief systems, other ways people choose to get steady on their feet as their day begins. Mine is to grab my Bible and a thermos of hot tea and head outside or, if I'm away from home, to a quiet corner. I believe this time with God sets the whole tone for my day. This habit helps me start my day with a clear mind that isn't wrapped around me.

I don't claim to be religious because I'm not. I do enjoy a relationship with Jesus. I love living in a country where we may openly speak about such choices and make them for ourselves. I've flown into countries where this is not the case.

Good habits become a personal gold mine and should be guarded as such. The reverse is also true: bad habits, which we all have, can become an anchor wrapped around our feet, dragging us down. Habits of all kinds can dictate our behavior every day when we let them. They will dictate our behavior in a time of crisis because, again, habits become instincts under pressure.

If you have ever played a sport or a musical instrument, you've heard the saying "You will play like you practice." It's that simple. Mental memory and muscle memory are real.

In a crisis, adrenaline brings clarity, but it can't expand your knowledge. It won't change your reasoning. Your existing reasoning simply works at hyper speed. In the moment, you won't experience an epiphany beyond what is already within you, what you have already taken time to learn or know.

For me, the realization that Darren and I might not be able to keep our aircraft together long enough to descend through 32,500 feet and land brought a clear thought to the front of my mind: perhaps this was the day I would meet my Maker face-to-face. My mind rushed to that conclusion but stopped short of that cliff of fear because I spend time with Jesus every day. I wouldn't be meeting a stranger.

The peace that followed that speed train of thought was the source of my calm voice, captured on the flight recorder while we shuddered and shook all the way down. I had no idea what had happened, no idea when something else might happen to send the aircraft out of control. But my habit of spending daily time with a God who loves me gave me a stillness and peace beyond reason. It steadied me.

A number of other habits served my crew and me well that day. The few minutes we had together before the flight, talking about things that were important to us, created a foundation of trust that we critically needed after that engine failed. The habits I had developed after years of flying, compartmentalizing, and training in aviation emergencies and out-of-control flights gave me a particular advantage. Darren and I already knew how to prioritize what needed our attention and when. So did our flight attendants. If we had to stop and think through every task, we wouldn't have accomplished our job that day. Some things had to be done instinctively, both inside and outside of the cockpit.

Sometimes I'm asked about my decision to walk through the cabin and speak to each person after Flight 1380 landed. This, too, is a habit of mine. When things aren't running smoothly, I try to alleviate the mysteries that can aggravate people.

Again, we act on what we believe. I believe in the worth of others—simply put, in the worth of human life. Whether I know a person has no bearing on his or her value. Every life is precious, made with purpose. I didn't come up with this idea; it's an ancient one that was taught to me by some great mentors, beginning with my parents. This belief affects the way I treat others, and my resulting habit of caring about others has become instinctive.

The second truth I've come to realize since the events of Flight 1380 is that hope may not change our circumstances, but it always changes us.

Hope, like habits, is uniquely human and, again, a gift. Our minds are incredibly powerful, and hope is the glue that holds us together when facts and circumstances could easily tear us apart.

During my SERE School training in Spokane, Washington, I heard story after incredible story about prisoners of war who had survived years of horrid treatment. What pulled them through? It wasn't hatred for their enemies, as is often popularly portrayed. Hatred rots us from within. Instead it was their minds, focused on a destination beyond the pain of that moment, that got them through each day. One gentleman played golf in his mind, hole by hole. Another made a pet of a spider, just to keep his mind wrapped around something other than his own circumstances. Playing mental golf, caring for a spider—these events became something the POWs looked forward to, something to engage their minds and hearts when their surroundings were unbearable.

Hope, even in a tiny dose, is powerful.

When hope is gone, even those who have good health and all the luxuries of the world can despair. Hope is something to look forward to, something to pull us through.

On a smaller scale, I learned early in life that carrots—little rewards—help to foster hope. I could get the little ones in children's choir to stop chatting and sing if they knew brownies awaited them after practice. I could convince naval aviators not to worry about the eerie feeling of losing control of the aircraft if they knew we would do aerobatics or sightseeing after the last spin of their out-of-control flight was finished.

That day on Flight 1380, when Darren suggested we go to Philadelphia and we agreed it was the right distance away and had the right runway and the right kind of ground support, our perspective on our bad situation shifted. We had a destination. We had hope.

When I shared that hope with the cabin over the PA, Rachel, Seanique, and Kathryn treated it like the treasure it was. They unbuckled and sacrificially reassured people. They shared their own oxygen masks at times, at their own peril.

Again, hope didn't change our circumstances one bit. We were on the same rough ride, with plenty of unanswered questions and unsolved mysteries staring us in the face. But when Darren and I knew where we were going, we could start working on a plan. As people accepted the truth that we weren't in an out-of-control free fall, hope started to calm everyone in an otherwise terrifying situation—to the point that we could all sidestep panic and do our best thinking.

No, hope won't necessarily change our circumstances, but it will change us.

The third truth I've come to recognize is that heroes do not require a title or equipment. They don't need to land a crippled plane. A true hero is someone who takes the time to see and makes the effort to act on behalf of someone else. In a word, they care.

For the past year I've stood in an unfamiliar spotlight because of what happened on Flight 1380, and I confess the attention makes me uncomfortable because I didn't act alone. I had years of training and preparation. I had an amazing crew in the cockpit, courageous flight attendants in the cabin, attentive air traffic controllers, caring passengers themselves, skilled first responders, and a strong team on the ground that acted quickly and with compassion.

During this time, I've found it intriguing that people covering the story have been more interested in how I treated people after the flight than in what it took to fly the crippled airplane safely to the ground. I'm encouraged to see that our culture still places such worth not on what people achieve but on how they demonstrate human kindness. This speaks to our country's values. We don't have a perfect country because we are not a perfect people. But we live in a land that values people, human life. This is a good country to live in. This focus on people shines a light on the true heroes all around us.

A lump still comes to my throat when I think of the bold and selfless acts that so many people displayed during the crisis. When I emerged from the cockpit, one of the first things I observed, after the remarkable sight of a composed and orderly cabin, was the way strangers were treating each other with the tenderness of a family. Later I learned more about what passengers Andrew Needum, Tim McGinty, and Peggy Phillips had done. The confirmation of how selfless people can be, how wonderful some really are, made me forget the previous half hour. These people didn't suddenly become compassionate or courageous. They had a history—they had developed a longstanding habit of loving others and acting unselfishly.

My crew—and I say "my" because I hope they say the same—showed their heroic habits as well. They were never passive or stunned into inactivity or silence. Freezing up would have been understandable, but their focus was never on themselves. It was on the mission at hand, on others.

Their amazing willingness to help others carried many through the stressful flight.

If we could replay a video of that day, you would see all the unsung heroes of the flight. Darren was so composed, an exceptional pilot as well as an extraordinary gentleman. A shot of the cabin would show our flight attendants acting without concern for themselves, always thinking ahead about how to best care for their customers, their people. There were other heroes on board that day, many who will never see their names or actions applauded in print. Even the passenger who knelt down and tied another person's shoelaces before leaving the aircraft is a hero worth noting.

How do we learn to behave this way toward each other?

We start with the knowledge that when we give a person time and attention, we give them influence. If we hold a person up as a hero, that person becomes part of the picture of what a hero looks like, what a hero does. Like habits, I strive to focus on the heroes and not be distracted by the villains.

Among my own heroes are people such as my dad, who passed

away while I was writing this book. I'm convinced it was my daddy who kept blinders off me while growing up, then encouraged me to tackle the nonsense in my path rather than avoid it when I grew older.

My mom is also my hero for too many reasons to list (as well as being the most selfless cheerleader I know).

Captain Rosemary Mariner was a mentor and friend of thirty years as well as a hero of mine who I also said farewell to this winter.

And the amazing man I married, Dean, is a hero whose selflessness continues to humble me and make me grateful.

"Whatever is true, whatever is noble, whatever is right, whatever is pure, whatever is lovely, whatever is admirable—if anything is excellent or praiseworthy—think about such things" (Philippians 4:8 NIV). As we hold on to what is true and noble, we'll know the worthy heroes when we see them.

Being a hero doesn't require a title or equipment. It does require a track record of selflessness and hope.

★ ★ ★

My dream of flying was only the starting pistol that launched me down the path of my life. It was the race that lay before me, the years of hard work without any guarantee of success, that put me in the right place at the right time, prepared to make a difference when I sat in the captain's seat on Flight 1380. Dreams aren't always just about us, but they start within our own hearts and minds.

As I've looked back over my life, I'm amazed at how the people and circumstances that were such challenges at the time—such as the two years it took me to find my way into the Navy—turned out to be what I believe are perfect examples of God's timing. If not for that two-year "delay," I doubt I would have met Dean. The F/A-18 wouldn't have been open to women. I would have missed making some of my lifelong friends. And I would have missed having two kids that give me such joy, knowing the world is a better place because they're here.

When one door closed, I simply knocked on another and then another until I found one unlocked. When I determined the direction of my quest, I still had to lower my shoulder and push as anyone does, guy or girl. When I would find myself in new territory, meeting resistance, I tried to step back and consider why I had been met with such a storm. The Socratic saying "The unexamined life is not worth living" took on personal meaning. *Which door should I push through? Did I have the right to be there? Were my motives honorable? Was I standing on my own merits?* If the answers were not obvious or forthcoming, I put the question before the One who made me.

I put my confidence in truth, including the truth of who I am: a woman created and loved by a God who isn't angry with me but crazy about me.

I think of the Olympic runner Eric Liddell, whose story was immortalized in the film *Chariots of Fire*. In the script Eric says, "God made me fast. And when I run, I feel His pleasure." That's how I feel about flying.

You might recall that when I was at the dreaming stage of aviation while still in high school, I ran across a poem called "To a Waterfowl," by William Cullen Bryant. Instead of going into the field of education or law, as his family and friends expected and encouraged him to do, Bryant wanted to write. He was torn. Should he follow sound advice or weigh his abilities and dreams, which were drawing him toward writing?

Back then I understood his dilemma. Today I feel the last stanza of the poem represents my life story in four short lines. Now I pass it on to you.

> He who, from zone to zone,
> Guides through the boundless sky thy certain flight,
> In the long way that [you] must tread alone,
> Will lead [your] steps aright.

Blessings in your adventures ahead.

With joy,

Captain Tammie Jo Shutts

QUICK REFERENCE GUIDE FOR MILITARY TERMINOLOGY

Naval Officer Ranks

- O-1: Ensign
- O-2: Lieutenant Junior Grade
- O-3: Lieutenant
- O-4: Lieutenant Commander
- O-5: Commander
- O-6: Captain
- O-7: Rear Admiral (one-star)
- O-8: Rear Admiral (two-star)
- O-9: Vice Admiral
- O-10: Admiral

Naval Squadron Leadership Positions

- CO: Commanding Officer
- XO: Executive Officer
- Ops O: Operations Officer
- MO: Maintenance Officer
- Admin: Administration Officer
- Safety: Safety Officer

Aviation Officer Candidate School Terms

- Batt: Battalion
- C-course: Cross-country course
- Dilbert Dunker: mock cockpit on a set of rails that runs down into a pool and flips over, used to train aircrew how to egress from a jet cockpit submerged and flipped underwater
- Helo Dunker: large barrel configured inside like a helicopter, used for training how to egress underwater from a submerged helicopter or one that is submerged and flipped
- Hop-and-pops: eight-count exercise consisting of a jumping jack, a squat thrust, and a push-up
- Maggot: all AOCs in the eyes of their drill instructors
- NAMI: Naval Aviation Medical Institute; the medical facility and group that checks all AOCS candidates to endorse their application as being medically qualified for flight status
- O-course: Obstacle course

Common Military Terms

- ACM: Air Combat Maneuvering
- ATC: Air Traffic Control
- BOQ: Bachelor Officer Quarters; military hotel for officers
- FCLP: Field Carrier Landing Practice; landing practiced on a runway before attempting to land on a carrier
- NAS: Naval Air Station
- SEAL: Sea, Air and Land; Navy special forces
- OCF: Out of Control Flight; flight to practice stalls and spins that requires a pilot aboard to regain control
- PT: Physical Training
- SERGRAD: Selectively Retained Graduate; pilot who receives wings and has required grade average or better who's invited to teach in one of the training squadrons

Aircraft Flown by Tammie Jo

- T-34 Mentor: Beechcraft single turbine engine, 550 horsepower
- T-2 Buckeye: also known as the Guppy, due to its looks, built by North American Rockwell and used for naval intermediate jet training
- A-4 Skyhawk: Douglas single-engine jet; an agile attack aircraft built in the 1950s and eventually used in naval advanced jet training
- A-7 Corsair: single-engine jet manufactured by Vought, replacing the Douglas A-4 Skyhawk

- F/A-18 Hornet: twin-engine fighter and attack jet built by McDonnell Douglas, replaced the A-7 Corsair
- O-2 Skymaster: twin-engine Cessna, used for spotting, or reconnaissance, in Vietnam and for forest firefighting
- Boeing 737 (200, 300, 500, 700, 800 series): fleet of commercial airliners flown by Southwest Airlines

Tammie Jo's Navy Flight Path

Orders	Squadron Assignments	Aircraft
AOCS	Aviation Officer Candidate School	
VT-27	Primary Flight Training Squadron	T-34 Turbo Mentor
VT-26	Intermediate Jet Training Squadron	T-2 Buckeye
VT-25	Advanced Jet Training Squadron	TA-4 Skyhawk
VT-26	SERGRAD Instructor	T-2 Buckeye
VAQ-34	Tactical Electronic Warfare Squadron	A-7 Corsair and F/A-18 Hornet
VA-122	Light Attack Training Squadron	A-7 Corsair
VFA-125	Strike Fighter Training Squadron	F/A-18 Hornet

ACKNOWLEDGMENTS

I would like to put a spotlight on a few individuals who made my story come to life on paper. To begin, Mel Berger and Mark Roesler believed my story was worth telling. The wonderful team at W Publishing, a division of Thomas Nelson, turned that vision into a tangible book. Daisy Hutton and Debbie Wickwire, ladies of literature, have my gratitude and admiration. Dean Shults is tireless as an editor and amazing in his clarity of details. Erin Healy's hard work and magical polish made the manuscript something I want my mom to read. There are many more people, unnamed, to whom I owe a sincere thank-you.

To my family, those who raised me in truth and love—thank you for pointing me toward the cherished source of such treasure.

To the family I raised—you refined my understanding of love even more. You changed my world.

To the man of my dreams—you're still by my side after thirty years of off-track, unscripted adventures. Thank you for remaining securely in my heart of hearts as we journey together. You are the man I love.

And to the One who created me on purpose, with a purpose—thank You for the gift of life.

ABOUT THE AUTHOR

Captain Tammie Jo Shults is a Southwest Airlines captain and former naval aviator who received wide acclaim when, on April 17, 2018, she and her crew successfully landed a Boeing 737 after a catastrophic engine failure and rapid depressurization, saving the lives of 148 people. Shults's early interest in flying led her to become one of the first female F/A-18 Hornet pilots in the United States Navy after overcoming several obstacles due to her gender. Her rare talent, uncommon history, and rich personal faith are the foundation of her inspirational life.